The Garden *of* Eden

Major and Malinda Cheney.
Sanders family collection.

The GARDEN *of* EDEN

The Story of a Freedmen's Community in Texas

by Drew Sanders

Library of Congress Cataloging-in-Publication Data

Sanders, Drew, 1947- author.
 The Garden of Eden : the story of a freedman's community in Texas / Drew Sanders.
   pages cm
 Includes bibliographical references and index.
ISBN 978-0-87565-620-5 (pbk.) – ISBN 978-0-87565-625-0 (hdbk.)
1. African Americans–Texas–Tarrant County–Biography. 2. Freedmen–Texas–Tarrant County–Biography. 3. African American families–Texas–Tarrant County–History. 4. Community life–Texas–Tarrant County–History. 5. Garden of Eden (Fort Worth, Tex.)–History. 6. Garden of Eden (Fort Worth, Tex.)–Biography. 7. Garden of Eden (Fort Worth, Tex.)–Genealogy. 8. African American neighborhoods–Texas–Tarrant County–History. 9. African American neighborhoods–Texas–Fort Worth–History. I. Title.
 F392.T25S26 2015
 305.896'0730764531–dc23
                         2015020113

TCU Press
TCU Box 298300
Fort Worth, Texas 76129
817.257.7822
www.prs.tcu.edu
To order books: 1.800.826.8911

Design by Barbara Mathews Whitehead

The author and TCU Press gratefully acknowledge the generous support of the Tarrant County Historical Society and XTO Energy toward the publication of this book.

In memory of
Dollie Cheney,
James "Dick Cheney" Sanders,
and A. J. "Buddy" Sanders

CONTENTS

Foreword by Bob Ray Sanders / ix
Acknowledgments / xiii

Introduction / 1
1 / The Loyds and the Long Road to Texas / 5
2 / Navidad Nation:
The Cheney Family in Lavaca County / 16
3 / Birdville: Setting the Stage for the Garden of Eden / 23
4 / Aunt Doll and the Sam Bass Stories:
Major Cheney Comes of Age / 35
5 / Early Life in the Garden of Eden / 40
6 / Other African American Communities in Tarrant County
and How They Relate to the Garden of Eden / 59
7 / The Cheney Children / 72
8 / Sand and Gravel / 86
9 / Unraveling:
A New Generation and Depressing Times / 96
10 / Use it up, Wear it out, Make it do . . . / 107
11 / A New Generation of Sanderses / 128
12 / Rebuilding Community in the Twenty-first Century / 149

Appendix: Family Connections / 162
Notes / 172
Bibliography / 191
Index / 194

Drew Sanders and his uncle, Bob Ray Sanders, were born only nine days apart, so they attended the same 1955 third-grade class at the African American Riverside Elementary School. This photograph shows the school's elementary choir. Both boys are in the second row, sixth and seventh from the left. Bob Ray is wearing a bow tie. Sanders family collection.

FOREWORD

As the name suggests, the Garden of Eden was always a fertile place, both in terms of its rich soil that produced bountiful vegetation for decades and in terms of the strong people who occupied the land.

But in contrast to its name—and despite the close-knit family ties that remain in place today—the garden was not always peaceful. That was due in part to it being territory in Tarrant County mostly occupied by black people, which neither Fort Worth nor Birdville (later Haltom City) wanted to claim.

By the time I came along, the last of James and Edith Sanders's twelve children, there was a conflict of cultures, with Texas and the South still under the heel of Jim Crow but clearly on the eve of change as the nation wrestled with the issue of segregation versus integration.

My conception, which I've always imagined came as a surprise for my parents, who were growing older and presumably had finished with having more babies, was miraculous in many ways. The first ten brothers and sisters had come two years apart. An eleventh child, Johnny Zero, came three years after the last child and lived for only a couple of days.

My birth, coming three years after Johnny, also came nine days after the birth of my oldest nephew, Andrew James Sanders Jr., my oldest brother's first child, who was known to many as "Bubba" and later as "Drew." Andrew was older than his uncle, but in truth we grew up more like brothers. To this day, many people consider him my brother or at the very least my cousin—the concept of uncle and nephew just doesn't register with them even after all these years.

We went through school together, bussed to Riverside Elementary and I. M. Terrell Junior-Senior High School in Fort Worth, which was one of the best things that could have happened to us. For in those all-black schools were some of the most educated, dedicated, caring, and loving teachers anywhere in the country, and they knew they were preparing us for the future—for the change that was on the horizon.

Even though there were schools much closer to home, including Birdville (Haltom) High, which literally was on our street, we could not go there. In hindsight, I'm very glad I didn't because there was no way people there (at that time in particular) could have prepared us, indeed armed us, for the challenges ahead.

But long before we ever got to a classroom, we had been steeped in the teachings of family, understanding from an early age that there was something special in that clan that had survived and flourished against incredible odds.

I was patriarch Major Cheney's great-grandson; Drew was his great-great-grandson, and we knew that we were part of a legacy that was still being built by my father and his. We grew up knowing the stories of how this was a family which, although descendants of a slave, had no fear of white people, and thus was a family in a position to help people of all colors. The hobos who rode the rails would often get off the trains at the crossing just a few miles east of downtown Fort Worth, as it was the nearest one to our house—which had been identified as a place they could always expect a handout.

Major Cheney, whose first name I've always had to explain was not a military title, was a living legend. Of course, I never thought I'd live to see a school named for him, but the Birdville ISD has done just that.

Drew and I understood that our parents and foreparents had been major landowners in Tarrant County, meaning that they paid many taxes on that land for over a century. Despite those tax dollars having been used to build schools, parks, public transportation, and other amenities, we could not use them at all, or those things that we could use were only allowed on a very limited and discriminatory basis.

Yes, we knew what it felt like to ride on the back of the bus, to be relegated to "Colored" water fountains, barred from the Fort Worth Zoo except one day out of the year, prohibited from jumping into the nearest public swimming pool at Sylvania Park, and required to ride a bus past several schools every day to get to one that would accept us.

Yet, the segregation and discrimination was not something our family dwelled on. They were too busy providing for their children and many other families who were in need. They were busy teaching us responsibility, a true work ethic, and the importance of an education.

Although I came along late—my older brothers and sisters insisted that I never had to work and never got punished the way they did—I was indeed introduced to chores at an early age. Drew and I herded cattle from the lot near the house to a pasture a quarter of a mile or half a mile away every morning before school, and drove them back again in the evening after school.

Of the forty acres my father still owned along the Trinity River during my youth, eight were reserved for a garden and raising hay to store for the cattle in the wintertime. Harvesting was part of everybody's job, including mine. Admittedly, I didn't do a lot, but I did my share.

I remember the falls in the pecan grove on that land, picking up pecans in the afternoons and on Saturdays, so that we could sell them to the Ellis Pecan shop on the North Side. That's how I made my Christmas money.

Both Drew and I were involved in many extracurricular activities at school, in the church, and in the community. He played football; I played in the band. No matter what we did, we were expected not just to achieve, but to excel.

And although I was the budding journalist, the one who was inquisitive and loved to report my findings, Drew always had a natural curiosity, especially when it came to family history. He did more interviewing of the elder family members than I did.

His passion for that genealogy never waned. In fact, he became more passionate as he got older, almost as if he were on an urgent mission to gather all the details before they somehow vanished and would be lost forever.

He spent the time in the libraries, researching old census records, traveling to places to connect with that "white" part of the family, and beginning to write it all down to preserve for future generations of the family.

He became the official griot—the keeper of our history, the storyteller, the attendant of the family flame, making sure it would never be extinguished or forgotten.

Drew has taught me and many others in the family details about our history that indeed would have been lost had it not been for his persistent and dedicated work and analysis.

This book tells that story of a family—and a community that grew up around it—whose ancestors shook off the shackles of slavery, refused to be cowed by prejudice and discrimination, and resisted the temptation to hate even those who sometimes hated them.

Drew's book tells the true tale of a family tree deeply rooted in a garden—*The Garden of Eden: The Story of a Freedmen's Community in Texas.*

And although it is a story of our family, it is one that should resonate with anyone who has a love for history, a sense of community, and a compassionate reverence for the triumph of the human spirit.

Bob Ray Sanders
November 3, 2014

ACKNOWLEDGMENTS

Wow, what a journey! An undertaking such as this has little hope of completion without the assistance of many generous people.

This book would not have been possible without the continuous conversations I had with my grandfather "Papa James," James McKinley Sanders Sr.; my aunt, Dollie Cheney; and A. J."Buddy" Sanders. They're all deceased now, but I owe them a great deal of gratitude for taking the time to talk about their parents, childhood experiences, and "growing up black in Birdville and Tarrant County."

Special thanks to the members of my family, which includes my aunts, uncles, sisters, brothers, Frank Howard, Hattie & Lilly Hooper, and more importantly, my wife and children, for believing that after more than thirty years of research our family history would be documented in this form. Thanks also to Nun Fretwell for sharing his stories with me.

I would like personally to express my gratitude to the extended family of Major Cheney who reside in Lavaca County. I had the pleasure of meeting with them in Hallettsville, Texas, and learning more about the history of the Cheney ancestors. During my visit, I met a policeman who pulled me over because he thought I was lost. He asked me who I was looking for, and I told him I was looking for my relatives, the Cheneys. He responded, "The only Cheneys in this town are white!" I responded, "They would be the ones." He became interested and proceeded to lead me to the local library, police station, and high school.

*A. J. "Drew" Sanders, the author, with Opal and Joe Woods's automobile,
circa 1955. Sanders family collection.*

After I'd been in town for more than two days, the white Cheneys came
by to inquire about the black Cheney. Needless to say, the visit was en-
lightening for both sides of the Cheney family.

I would like to acknowledge the following individuals and organizations for their contributions to this book: the Fort Worth Library's Ge-
nealogy and Archives Department, Tom Kellam and the Heritage Room
at Tarrant County College Northeast, the Portal to Texas History, the
Handbook of Texas Online, Cathy Belcher and the *Fort Worth Star-
Telegram*, Cathy Spitzenberger and the University of Texas at Arlington
Special Collections, Tom Shelton and Carlos Cortez at the University
of Texas at San Antonio, Anne Peterson and Katie Dziminski in the De-
Golyer Library at Southern Methodist University, Carole Compton
Glenn, Robert Ray, Bob Bell, and Robert McCubbin at *True West* mag-

azine, Adrianne Pierce and the Texas/Dallas History & Archives Division of the Dallas Public Library, the Fort Worth Independent School District—Billy W. Sills Center for Archives, Mark Thomas and the Birdville Independent School District, Sylvia Komatsu and Therese Powell at KERA, Patrick Walsh and the Texas General Land Office, Marie Grigsby, Constance Cooley and the Southlake Historical Society, and Tommy P. Cox and the Tarrant County Clerk's office. Thanks, also, to Hasson Diggs for documenting our family's 2015 Easter Sunday dinner, to Larry Schuessler for his assistance in scanning family photographs, and to Carol Zuber-Mallison for crafting the Tarrant County map that shows the location of the Garden of Eden and other sites important to our family.

Finally, thank you, Carol Roark and TCU Press. I am most grateful to Carol for her hard work, thorough editing skills, and sage advice in the ultimate completion of this family legacy. Thank you, TCU Press, for pursuing an interest in our family history and documenting it for future generations.

Thank you for making my dream become a reality.

Drew Sanders
September 30, 2014

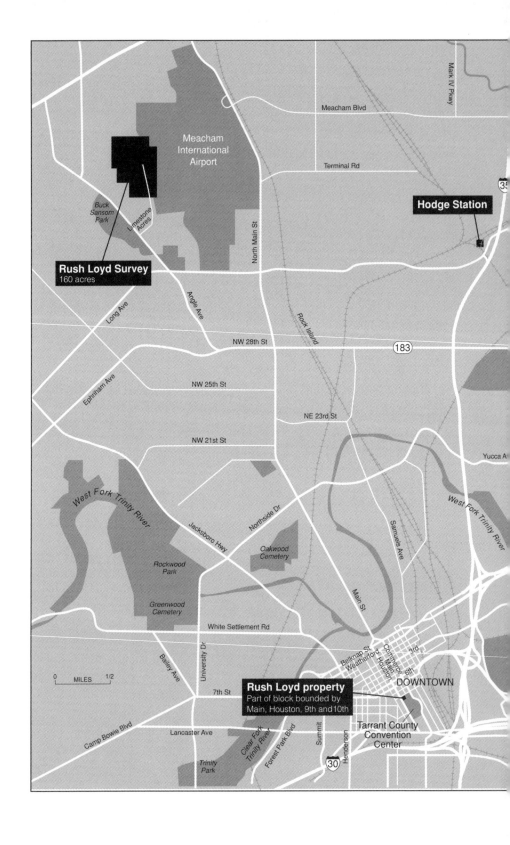

Meacham Blvd

Mark IV Pkwy

Meacham
International
Airport

Terminal Rd

North Main St

Hodge Station

35

Buck
Sansom
Park

Limestone
Acres

Rush Loyd Survey
160 acres

Long Ave

Angle Ave

Rock Island

NW 28th St

183

Ephriham Ave

NW 25th St

NE 23rd St

NW 21st St

Yucca A

West Fork Trinity River

Jacksboro Hwy

Northside Dr

Oakwood
Cemetery

West Fork Trinity River

Samuels Ave

Rockwood
Park

Main St

Greenwood
Cemetery

White Settlement Rd

University Dr

Belknap St
Weatherford
Commerce
Main
Houston
3rd
6th

DOWNTOWN

0   MILES   1/2

Bailey Ave

7th St

Rush Loyd property
Part of block bounded by
Main, Houston, 9th and 10th

Tarrant County
Convention
Center

Camp Bowie Blvd

Lancaster Ave

Clear Fork Trinity River

Forest Park Blvd

Summit

Henderson

30

Trinity
Park

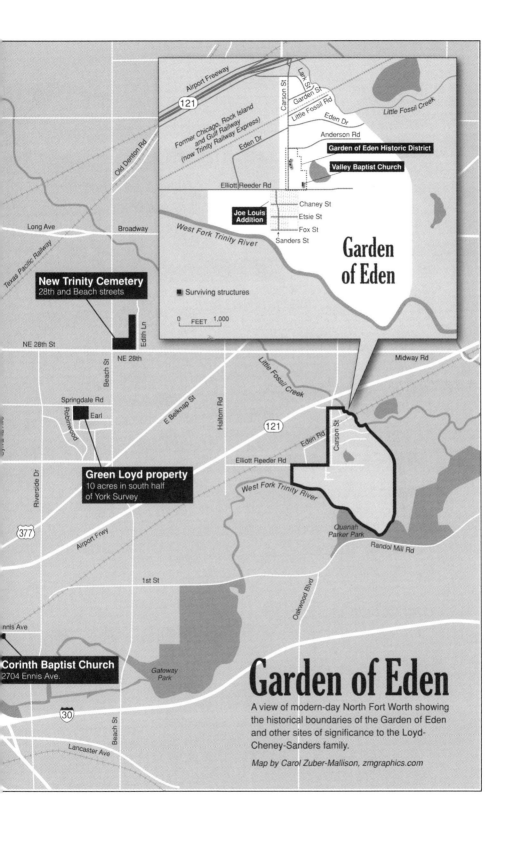

New Trinity Cemetery
28th and Beach streets

Airport Freeway

121

Former Chicago, Rock Island
and Gulf Railway
(now Trinity Railway Express)

Carson St

Lark St

Garden St

Little Fossil Rd

Eden Dr

Little Fossil Creek

Anderson Rd

Garden of Eden Historic District

Valley Baptist Church

Eden Dr

Elliott Reeder Rd

Joe Louis Addition

Chaney St

Etsie St

Fox St

Sanders St

West Fork Trinity River

Garden of Eden

Long Ave

Broadway

Texas Pacific Railway

Old Denton Rd

NE 28th St

Edith Ln

Surviving structures

0   FEET   1,000

NE 28th

Beach St

NE 28th

Midway Rd

Springdale Rd

Robinwood

Earl

E Belknap St

Haltom Rd

Little Fossil Creek

121

Eden Rd

Carson St

Elliott Reeder Rd

Green Loyd property
10 acres in south half
of York Survey

West Fork Trinity River

Riverside Dr

377

Airport Frwy

Quanah
Parker Park

Randol Mill Rd

1st St

Oatwood Blvd

nnis Ave

Corinth Baptist Church
2704 Ennis Ave.

Gateway
Park

Garden of Eden

A view of modern-day North Fort Worth showing
the historical boundaries of the Garden of Eden
and other sites of significance to the Loyd-
Cheney-Sanders family.

Map by Carol Zuber-Mallison, zmgraphics.com

30

Lancaster Ave

Beach St

Valley Baptist Church in the Garden of Eden after an April 13, 2007, tornado tore off the roof and flattened walls. Sanders family collection.

INTRODUCTION

C urving northeast, the tornado slammed into the tiny neighborhood, flattening the church and peeling siding and roofs off the houses. Much had already been lost in the tiny enclave—when gravel pits stripped away the bottomland and the big house burned—but this 2007 disaster and the havoc it wreaked sparked the rebirth of one of Tarrant County's oldest communities. It isn't a town—like Fort Worth or Arlington or even Grapevine—regularly found on Texas maps, but an African American family enclave founded more than 130 years ago just south of the old farming community of Birdville, and now found on Carson Street in the northeast part of Fort Worth, Texas. This is the story of the Garden of Eden and the people who made this rich pocket of Trinity River bottomland a vibrant and resilient place.

People of African descent have been a part of the western migration and settlement of this country, and no true history of Texas can be written without including them. Yet, for many years, the story of the state was told with only a passing reference to "slaves" as a group and no mention of individuals or their accomplishments. There were relatively few slaves or free people of color in the area that would become Texas under Spanish rule.[1] Indeed, during the first decade of the nineteenth century, the total population hovered between three thousand and seven thousand souls, with only a few hundred slaves. Both Spain and Mexico offered slaves legal means to buy their freedom and escape bondage. The picture began to change when Spain opened Texas to Anglo colonization in 1820. After Mexico gained independence from Spain in 1821, more and more settlers brought slaves with them when they moved to Texas, counting on the Mexican government to turn a blind eye despite an official policy prohibiting bondage. On the eve of the Texas Revolution, in 1836, there were about twenty thousand people of Anglo descent in Texas, approximately five thousand slaves, and only a few hundred Native Americans.[2]

The slave population increased dramatically once Texas became independent and the Republic of Texas reverted to policies that treated slaves as property, not people. By 1840 there were an estimated thirteen thousand slaves, and the republic also prohibited free people of color from migrating to the new nation. The number of slaves more than quadrupled, to a bit over fifty-eight thousand by 1850, five years after Texas entered the Union as a slave state.[3] On the eve of the Civil War in 1860, the number of slaves in Texas had surged to 169,000, and only 350 to 700 free people of color, out of a total population of 604,215.[4]

The Cheney family—both whites and the enslaved blacks that they owned—migrated to Texas in the early 1830s, while it was still part of Mexico. The Loyd family, again both white and enslaved people of color, was the first group in this story to arrive in Tarrant County. They settled on land next to the area that would become the Garden of Eden, just as the Civil War was getting under way. Malinda Loyd Cheney was born on the Loyd property in 1862, and members of the Cheney-Sanders family still live today on land that is immediately adjacent to the former holdings of the white Loyd family. The Boaz family, a third group that developed ties to the Cheney and Loyd families through marriage and shared their efforts to build a community, arrived in Texas as slaves of Samuel Boaz in 1859. (Variant spellings, particularly the spelling of proper names, appear frequently in nineteenth-century records. This volume uses the family's traditional spellings for Loyd and Cheney, but many of the records cited use the variant spellings of Lloyd and Chaney for both the white and African American family members.

The family also had a number of nicknames for various family members—but in order to reduce confusion, a standard name format has been used for each person. For example, Major Cheney was called "Mage" throughout his adult life, but his grandson Major Guerry was also called "Mage." Thus, their nicknames are not used.)

Although the story of the early years of white settlement in Texas has focused on the actions of whites and, to some degree, the Tejanos who shaped life in the nation and state, the largely nameless people of African descent labored in obscurity. The slaves owned by the Cheney and Loyd families provided labor for farming and ranching operations, but they also learned skills that would stand them in good stead once they were free. The day-to-day life that slaves lived depended on the attitude of their masters. Although records are sketchy, indications are that both the Cheney and Loyd families cared for their slaves and treated them well. Even after their slaves were freed, the families maintained a cordial relationship with their former slaves and, at times, assisted them with legal and other affairs. Major Cheney was even asked to provide testimony about the white Cheney family in a proof of heirship document after Eliza J. Cheney died.[5]

Abraham Lincoln signed the Emancipation Proclamation in 1863 but, for Texas slaves, news of their freedom did not come until June 19, 1865, several weeks after the Civil War had ended. Because of this, June 19 is widely celebrated by African Americans not only in Texas but all over the United States as a day celebrating freedom.

Once they gained their freedom, working was not an option. Liberty gave these strong-willed individuals the opportunity to be responsible for their own actions and build a good life for their families. The Loyd and Boaz families began to build a viable community in the Garden of Eden, clearing river-bottom land that was covered with brush and located in the flood plain, so that they could plant crops and make their own living. Major Cheney moved to the area about 1879 and married

Malinda Loyd in 1881, beginning a family that would become the core of the Garden of Eden.

Nearby, other former slaves also established what came to be called "freedmen's settlements" or communities in Mosier Valley, Dove, Stop Six, Bear Creek, Egypt, North Dallas, Quakertown, and Pelham, in North Texas, as well as in other places throughout the eastern part of the state. They built churches and schools and, in some communities, eventually opened businesses that served the African American population.

For the Loyd and Cheney families, as well as the Boaz and other African Americans who lived in or near the Garden of Eden, it proved to be a fertile land that could produce everything the community needed, and a place where no one would be expelled. Perseverance, persistence, and the fruit of their labor reversed most of the memories of the hardships they once endured. Although they prospered in the earthly Garden of Eden, the families also remembered the significance of the Bible and the paradise it promised for those who believed in God and gave their lives to the Lord. Today, the extended family members still work to preserve not only the history of this special and sacred place, but to rebuild that which has been lost and share the story of the people who lived here before them and worked to make the land a true Garden of Eden.

CHAPTER 1

The Loyds and the Long Road to Texas

Now part of Fort Worth, the Garden of Eden is an enclave that nurtured eight generations of a family with a storied past. Woven from threads that form the fabric of American history—migration, slavery, free people of color, ranching, military service, farming, and mining—the story of the Loyd, Cheney, and Sanders families is a tale of both survival and success.

The Loyd family was the first to arrive in Tarrant County, coming as slaves during the Civil War. Green Loyd was born a slave about 1833 in Mercer County, Kentucky. Before 1867, he is not recorded by name in any official records. Prior to emancipation, the only reason for the government to keep track of individuals was for tax purposes and the decennial census. Slaves were considered property, so they were only listed by age and sex. In 1867, during Reconstruction, however, African Americans in Texas first gained the right to vote when Congress passed laws related to the Confederate states that had not ratified the Fourteenth Amendment.[1] The 1867 Tarrant County poll tax list is divided into two sections, one for "white polls" and one for "colored polls." Green Loyd appears on the "colored poll" list—an indication that he had paid the one-dollar state poll tax and the fifty-cent county poll tax in order to be able to exercise his newly acquired right to vote.[2]

Following the thin trail of records back to Kentucky reveals the story of a man who, though he could neither read nor write, was the first member of the African American Loyd family to come to Tarrant County, own land, raise a family, and live a life that touches on many of the themes in Texas history. A key to Green Loyd's story is found in the 1870 census, where he is listed with his wife and children in Tarrant County, living next door to Hale C. and Rebecca W. Loyd, near Birdville. The birthplaces of Green Loyd's children, as well as the birthplace of his wife Charlotte, track with the places that the white family of Hale and Rebecca Loyd lived: Kentucky, Mississippi, Missouri, and Texas.[3] Another clue to Green's history comes from an 1890 newspaper story,[4] which notes that Green Loyd, an "aged negro" (Loyd would have been fifty-seven at the time), had been accidentally shot by a man "who used to be his master in slavery times." The shooter, Leslie Mayes, was a member of the white branch of the Loyd family.[5]

Green Loyd's link with the white Loyd family begins with Hale C. Loyd, who was born in 1797 in Virginia. In 1822 he married Rebecca Bottoms,[6] a Kentucky native, and the couple lived and farmed in Mercer County, Kentucky, her home county. The 1830 census shows that the couple owned no slaves—the only other household member was a white male child less than nine years of age. This was likely a son who died in childhood, as he disappears from all later records. In December 1834, the Loyds welcomed twin boys into their family, Martin B. and Thomas P. Loyd. By 1840, the Loyds' property holdings had increased substantially. They owned land and three slaves—two females and one male. The male was very likely Green, who took his master's surname. Hale and Rebecca Loyd appear to have acquired Green Loyd when he was a boy between seven and ten years of age. Martin and Thomas Loyd were about the same age and likely played with Green Loyd, but only Hale Loyd and the male slave are listed as working in agriculture. The twins were pursuing an education, not working in the fields.

The lure of land and the opportunity it offered finally pulled the Loyds out of Kentucky. Newly available land in Chickasaw County, Mississippi, drew many settlers. It became available in the late 1830s, when the Chickasaw Indians who had lived there were forcibly removed and the land offered for sale. Land prices as low as twelve cents an acre led to a population increase from 2,148 people in 1840 to 9,887 people in 1850. The figure for the slave population is even more telling. It jumped from 807 individuals in 1840 to 6,480 in 1850.[7] Those numbers tell the story of the cotton culture, with slaves needed to make the backbreaking work of raising cotton profitable. Hale Loyd moved to Chickasaw County about 1846, so he and his family and their holdings were part of the population boom. He was not a large slaveholder by typical area standards. Most slaveholders there worked forty to fifty slaves while Hale Loyd had only ten slaves in 1850, three of them under the age of ten. One of the female slaves was likely a woman named Charlotte, who was born in Kentucky about 1843 and became Green Loyd's wife. Another, a male child, was Green's younger brother, Rush Loyd, born about 1855. Chickasaw County was a place where slaves were put to hard, productive work, but plantation farming needed a large labor force, and Hale Loyd did not have enough slaves to make such a situation work.

Mississippi did not provide everything that Hale Loyd wanted, so the family packed up and made a long and difficult journey through the South, crossing the Mississippi River by barge. In later years, Malinda Loyd Cheney recalled that the journey was so tough that some members of the family wanted to turn around and go back to Mississippi. The Loyds settled in Missouri for a few years during the mid-to-late 1850s. Green and Charlotte Loyd's eldest child, Henry, was born there. Their next move was a bit more surprising.

West Texas was a raw frontier in the late 1850s. While earlier settlers had worked with the Native American tribes in the area, a growing population of newcomers brought conflict over land and a flurry of Indian attacks. Palo Pinto County, organized in 1857, was the unstable region where the Loyd family chose to first set down.[8] Census records show that in 1860, Hale Loyd was a stock raiser in Palo Pinto County who

Tarrant county
December 1 1851

James. R. Shaw Esq
Comptroller Austin

Sir I here send you
a map of the town of Birdsville in
Tarrant county as the law requires me so to
I have only 4½ of State revenue on hand
at this time I have not received the opi
of the Attorney General that you prom
to send me on the case of the Settler
at Fort Worth I am in very Ba
helth at this time
Very Respectfey You
John. A. Hurst ass &c

This plat map showed the layout of Birdville in 1851. Main Street is now Carson Street, but the street was not extended south to the Garden of Eden until 1911. Courtesy of Texas State Library and Archives Commission.

owned $16,180 (almost half a million in 2013 dollars) in personal property. He was assisted by his son Martin. For whatever reason—Hale Loyd's increasing age, difficulty with Native American tribes, troubles as Texas grappled with the impact of secession, or a desire to be closer to more settled country—most of the Loyd clan moved to the Birdville area in Tarrant County about 1862. Martin Bottom Loyd

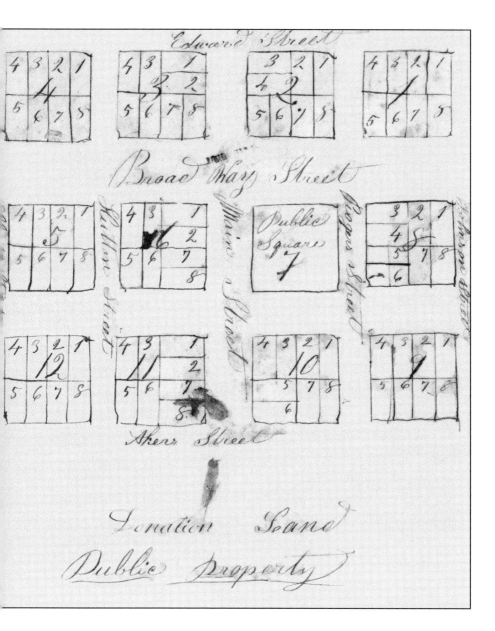

remained in Palo Pinto County to run the cattle operations, and accounts indicate that this business formed the foundation of M. B. Loyd's substantial fortune.[9]

Green Loyd and his family accompanied the white Loyd family to Texas and probably worked in the cattle business alongside Hale and M. B. Loyd. Charlotte and Green's family also began to grow. Two daughters, Eliza and Julia, are listed on the 1870 census as being born in Texas before the Civil War began.

When Texas seceded from the United States, Texans living in the less settled western part of the state faced the reality that federal troops would no longer be available to protect them from Indian attacks. The Confederacy didn't have the capacity to provide that protection and was much more focused on major battles with Union troops to the east. To fill the gap, the state of Texas enlisted citizens, largely drawn from the frontier counties that needed protection, and formed what came to be called the Frontier Regiment.[10] M. B. Loyd, who was going back and forth between his cattle interests in Palo Pinto County and family members settled near Birdville, "mustered in" or joined Company E of the Frontier Regiment commanded by Colonel James E. McCord on December 20, 1862, at Camp Salmon.[11] The Frontier Regiment troops followed the rules established for Confederate troops and were seen by the general public as part of the Confederate war effort, even though they were paid (or sometimes not paid) by the state of Texas rather than the Confederate States.

Serving in defense of the frontier was not a full-time occupation. Texas realized that the Frontier Regiment soldiers also needed to tend their crops and cattle, so the soldiers rotated duties—serving for a time in the field fighting Indians or rounding up Confederate deserters who sought refuge in the sparsely populated "brush country"—and then returning home for a period.[12] M. B. Loyd was promoted from lieutenant to captain on March 14, 1863, receiving the title that he would keep for the remainder of his life.[13]

The Frontier Regiment had trouble keeping soldiers. There were many deserters, either because men wanted to be at home to protect their property, didn't want to fight at all, or because they wanted to fight for the Confederacy rather than a homespun militia. The state of Texas sought to transfer control of the unit to the Confederacy, but insisted

M. B. Loyd came to Texas about 1860 with his parents, Hale and Rebecca Loyd, and his twin brother, Thomas P. Loyd.
The family first settled in Palo Pinto County but moved to Tarrant County when the Civil War began. Loyd and his parents owned slaves who would settle the Garden of Eden. He remained friends with the African American Loyd family after slavery ended and assisted them with business and legal affairs.
Courtesy DeGolyer Library, Southern Methodist University.

on safeguards to ensure that the troops would not be removed from frontier defense and sent to fight further east. In the meantime, the Texas government also sought additional soldiers on the frontier and in adjacent counties.

Surprisingly, another member of the Loyd family mustered in at Camp Salmon a few months after M. B. joined the Frontier Regiment. G. W. Loyd, a private, joined the same unit headed by Captain Loyd, part of Company E commanded by Colonel James E. McCord. The summary muster roll card prepared from Texas State Library archival holdings indicates that G. W. Loyd shelled corn for the regiment and served as a company teamster, taking care of the regiment's horses. M. B. Loyd was also G. W.'s mustering officer when he mustered out of the unit in November 1863.[14] There is no indication of race on the muster roll card, but the man's duties—which would not have required him to carry a firearm—and the close association with M. B. Loyd suggest that the person who served may have been Green Loyd. Both men were about the same age—twenty-eight or twenty-nine years old—a bit older than the prime age for military service in the regular Confederate troops.

Green Loyd's service with the Frontier Regiment would make him one of the first Buffalo Soldiers—the African American troops that served as Indian fighters on the western frontier. Unfortunately, he never spoke about his role in this part of American history, so the essence of the story must be pieced together from the sparse regimental records. Captain M. B. Loyd's troops did engage Indians in battle on several occasions. In July of 1863, Captain Loyd led his men on patrol out of Camp Colorado. They discovered signs that Indians were in the area and, with reinforcements from Camp Cooper, engaged them in a running battle. The Indians were able to escape, however, while Loyd waited for additional reinforcements and fresh horses.[15]

The state of Texas finally turned the Frontier Regiment over to the Confederacy on March 1, 1864, following an extended negotiation with the Confederacy to make certain that they would keep troops on the frontier to protect settlers.[16] Although muster roll records seem to show that Green Loyd was separated from service at this time, a fascinating piece of evidence indicates that he may have transferred from state to Confederate forces at some point. A circa 1901-1902 photograph titled "Officers and Force of First National Bank, Fort Worth" provides the intriguing clue. M. B. Loyd, the bank president, stands among a group of men identified by name and position in the bank. The photograph includes two African American men. One of them, Dallas Massay—who is holding a broom—is identified as the bank's porter. The other is Green Loyd—identified as "Greene Loyd"—and he is called an "Ex-Confederate."[17] Black Confederates are few and far between, but they did exist in Texas. In some situations, slaves accompanied their masters to the front to act as servants. Confederate enlistment records do show M. B. Loyd,[18] but no records have yet been found for Green Loyd. It is possible that Texans did not differentiate between those serving in the Frontier Regiment and those enlisted specifically with the Confederacy, rather seeing both efforts as part of service to the Confederacy. Regardless, the photograph indicates that M. B. Loyd maintained a relationship with Green Loyd after Hale Loyd died, and that Green Loyd's military service during the Civil War was recognized.

Green and Charlotte Loyd's family continued to grow after the Civil War started. Malinda Loyd, who plays a major role in this story, was born on November 9, 1862.[19] Family memories indicate that she was born in Tarrant County, not Palo Pinto County, and that seems plausible given the family's timeline in Texas. Malinda was the last member of the African American Loyd family born into slavery. Her sister Emma and brothers Lee and Martin were born in 1866 and 1869, respectively. In 1870, Green Loyd lived next door to Hale Loyd near Birdville and was likely farming his former owner's land. Hale Loyd was seventy-three and probably in declining health, as he died on December 24, 1871.[20]

Officers and Force of the First National Bank, Fort Worth, circa 1901-1902.
M. B. Loyd, president of the bank, stands in front of the counter on the center
right wearing a coat and tie. Green Loyd, who stands on the far right,
was a slave owned by the white Loyd family. His presence in this photograph,
where he is the only person who is not an employee, suggests that the bond
between the white and black Loyd families was still strong long after slavery
ended. The notation under his name on the photograph mount indicates
that Green Loyd had served with Confederate forces. Leslie Mayes, second
from the left behind the counter, was M. B. Loyd's nephew and the
person who accidentally shot Green Loyd in 1890.
Courtesy UTSA Libraries Special Collections.

Hale Loyd's sons were not involved in farming—Thomas P. Loyd, who became a physician, died in 1868, and Martin B. Loyd was gathering cattle that wandered western rangelands and sending them up the cattle trails to market.[21] M. B. Loyd also raised horses, necessary for herding and driving cattle, and was building up his land holdings. The 1873 Tarrant County property tax rolls show that M. B. Loyd owned 200 horses worth $2,000 and land worth $9,970.[22]

Green Loyd and his family did much better than many freed slaves. Though sketchy, newspaper and photographic evidence suggests that he maintained a cordial relationship with the white Loyd family, which likely provided benefits for him and for his family. Property tax rolls show that before he owned land, he owned horses, which were essential for farming or cattle operations. The 1871 tax rolls showed that he owned five horses worth fifty dollars (over $960 in 2013 dollars), and an additional eight dollars in miscellaneous property (quite likely tools).[23] By 1872, that group of five horses was worth $114.[24] Loyd was able to acquire land in 1885 when he purchased ten acres in the southern section of the John B. York Survey, just southwest of Birdville, and approximately two and a half miles northeast of Fort Worth.[25] Today his land would be roughly where Amon Carter Riverside High School is now located. He farmed for a living, first for others and then for himself. Green and Charlotte Loyd raised eleven children in Texas, including daughter Malinda Loyd, who would become the matriarch of the full-fledged Garden of Eden following her marriage to Major Cheney in 1881.

CHAPTER 2

Navidad Nation:
The Cheney Family in Lavaca County

The story of the Cheney family—at least the white branch of the family—is one that parallels many other Texas settlers eager for free land and a fresh start. John Cheney Sr. and his wife, Rachel Benson Cheney, lived in Anne Arundel County, Maryland, where he farmed. The couple had at least eight children before Rachel Cheney died about 1801. One son, John Richard "Dick" Cheney Jr. (hereafter referred to as Dick Cheney), named for his father, was born in 1796.[1]

Shortly after Rachel's death, John Cheney Sr. moved to Georgia with most of the children in tow. There he found a new wife, Catherine Evans Owen, whom he married in 1803. Settling in Green County, he began to acquire land and slaves and, with his new wife, to produce a second family. The large family meant that there were many mouths to feed and the need for a strong sense of family loyalty.

Dick Cheney, the fourth son from his father's first marriage, was born in Maryland. He married his first wife, Lucy Evans Owen, about 1817. She was reportedly of Native American ancestry, and the couple and their children (Mary, Lewis Rabon, Francis Marion, and John G.) moved to Texas about 1832, two years after the Indian Removal Act was passed.[2] The act proposed to provide land west of the Mississippi in exchange for Native American lands in Georgia, but the net effect was to force many families from their homes.[3] It appears that the Cheney family left ahead of the major removal push and settled in Texas rather than Indian Territory, thus negating any future claims regarding their status as Native Americans.

Unfortunately, the family arrived only a few years before the Texas Revolution and were caught up in its maelstrom. Lucy Evans Owen died in 1836 as the family was evacuating toward the Gulf Coast, trying to outrun the Mexican Army during the Runaway Scrape.[4] The remaining family members later returned home to what was then Colorado County (Lavaca County was formed in 1846 out of Colorado County), making them some of the first permanent settlers in the region. In January 1838 and May 1839, Dick Cheney made application for a league and a labor of land (approximately 4,605 acres total) along the north side of a bend in the Navidad River, affirming that he was a citizen of the Republic of Texas and had resided in Texas prior to May 1, 1835. He patented the land in 1841.[5] In 1846 he married his second wife, Charlotte Shaw, who died only a few years later, in 1849, after having given birth to three additional Cheney children.

Cheney's sons also acquired land, bringing the family's holdings in the area to almost seven thousand acres, which were farmed using at least some slave labor.[6] Both John (and the records are not clear whether it was John Richard "Dick" Cheney or John G. Cheney) and Lewis Rabon Cheney owned slaves. John Cheney is shown as owning a forty-six-year-old male, a twenty-six-year-old female, a two-year-old female, and a one-year-old male in the 1850 Lavaca County, Texas Slave Schedule, and Lewis Rabon Cheney owned a nineteen-year-old female, a fourteen-year-old female, and a one-year-old male, according to the 1860 Lavaca County, Texas Slave Schedule. Lavaca County historian Doug Kubicek indicates that the Cheney family would sometimes rent slaves from Washington Green Lee Foley, one of the county's largest

John Richard "Dick" Cheney Jr.'s 1841 land grant lay along the Navi-
dad River in Lavaca County, southeast of Hallettsville. By the time
this map was drawn in 1853 by Charles W. Pressler, Dick Cheney
had substantially increased his land holdings.
Major Cheney, his son by a slave woman, was born in this area
in 1856. Detail of map 3801,
Courtesy Texas General Land Office, Austin.

owners with 124 bondsmen in 1860, to increase their work force when needed.[7]

The Cheneys' land marked the start of an area that historian and author Paul C. Boethel called the "Navidad Nation." Situated along the bottomlands of the Navidad River between the Cheney settlement and today's community of Speaks, west of State Highway 530, this secluded area was filled with a bramble of vegetation and abundant wildlife. It was easy to get lost, and more than one person chose this place to distance themselves from the law or others that they did not want to encounter.[8] Dick Cheney was the patriarch of this place, and indications are that his character meshed with the freewheeling spirit that permeated the Navidad Nation. While the Cheneys did farm some of their land, given the small number of slaves they owned, it is likely that they also relied on cattle to produce income. Many reports characterize Dick Cheney as a scoundrel, a person who was more than willing to round up cattle and horses and call them his own, except when he conveniently forgot to list them for tax purposes.

In 1856, Dick Cheney was sixty years old, twice widowed, and the father of at least eight children, most of whom were fully grown. He wasn't finished with his family yet, however. On April 22, 1856, a slave woman gave birth to Major Cheney, the seventh son of Dick Cheney. The slave woman's name has been lost to history. She might have been one of the women owned by John or Lewis Rabon Cheney, or rented from another owner—the records simply don't give any clues. The practice of whites fathering mulatto children was common during this time. In 1860, for example, there were more than fifty mulatto children in Lavaca County under the age of ten, out of a total slave population of 1,606, and some listed as Negro may actually have been mulatto.[9] Most white fathers did not acknowledge their biracial children but, as bad as relationships were between the races, Dick Cheney reportedly did, giving his son his freedom and his name.[10] Free blacks were unusual in

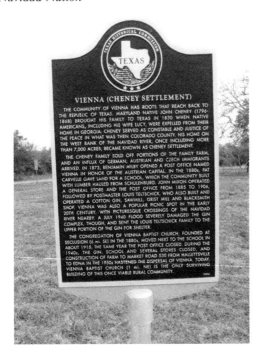

Echoes of the Cheney family's presence in Lavaca County still resonate. This historical marker commemorates the Cheney Settlement and the subsequent area community called Vienna. Sanders family collection.

Texas. In 1860, with a slave population of 182,566, there were only about four hundred free people of color.[11]

Major was raised by the Cheney family, but government records concerning his early life are nonexistent. He probably worked from the time he was first able, gaining both farming and cattle-raising skills. His story comes from family accounts, which indicate that he was closest to John G. Cheney, who was the white son of Dick and Lucy Cheney. John G. Cheney served as Justice of the Peace in Colorado County in 1843 and married Elizabeth "Eliza" Watts in 1848.

Lavaca County thrived during the 1850s, increasing in population from 1,571 in 1850 to 5,945 in 1860. Cotton farming began to supplant smaller-scale farming and cattle raising as the slave population increased.

Although there were shortages and the market for goods was limited during the Civil War, no battles were fought in Lavaca County, and cotton picked by slaves was still a profitable commodity. Like many of the white male southerners in Lavaca County, John G. Cheney became a Confederate soldier, enlisting at Hallettsville, Texas, on March 1, 1862, as part of Company M, Twenty-seventh Regiment, Texas Cavalry, under the command of John W. Whitfield. He enlisted as a private but left service as a sergeant.[12] The absence of white adult males also meant that those left behind had more work to do—and the Cheneys did not have enough slaves to give white family members a life of leisure.

Life in Lavaca County changed drastically following the Civil War. Property values plummeted, and white landowners scrambled to think of ways to keep their now-freed slaves working. Violence turned out to be one of the most often-used tools. Between 1865 and 1868, there were 939 murders committed in Texas. Of those, 429 were African Americans killed by whites. In contrast, only ten whites were murdered by African Americans. Given the breakdown in civil authority, few of these murders were prosecuted.[13] Predictably, there was more violence in rural areas, where most of the newly emancipated people of color lived. Lavaca County was no exception.

Former Confederates were loath to accept "Yankee rule," though the presence of federal troops was short lived. W. H. Heistead, a Freedmen's Bureau agent in Lavaca County, wrote to his superior in 1867 that "Free men in many cases are still ruled by revolver and bowie [sic] knife."[14] At first, the violence involved primarily cattle rustlers and horse thieves. Many of these gang members met up in the Navidad Nation to divide up their plunder, and it "became the favored haunt of the most violent citizens in the area."[15]

Family patriarch Dick Cheney died in 1868, doubtless adding to the stress the family was probably experiencing.[16] In 1869, life became even more difficult for Lavaca County freedmen as the gangs began to target and harass people of color.[17] At the time, Major Cheney would have been about thirteen years old, not a grown man but no longer a child, and a potential target for the gangs that ranged through the Navidad Nation. As a free person, it would have made sense for him to leave, but his family was here.

CHAPTER 3

Birdville:
Setting the Stage for the Garden of Eden

Prior to and during the Civil War, during a time of significant migration to Texas, there were two white families who moved to Northeast Tarrant County with their slaves, the Loyds and the Boazes. Samuel and Agnes Boaz arrived in Tarrant County during the early 1860s, at about the same time as the Loyd family. Samuel was originally from Virginia and Agnes from North Carolina, but the two married in Kentucky and moved to the Birdville area from that state. In 1850, the couple owned one slave, so it is probable that they brought one or more slaves with them a decade later.[1] The Loyds arrived in Texas with eleven slaves, including Green and Charlotte Loyd.[2] Newspapers and Kentucky neighbors who had moved to Texas before them extolled the opportunities that Texas would provide, and land described as productive was still plentiful.

The January 1, 1859, issue of the *Texas State Gazette* (Austin) paraphrases an article from the *Birdville Union* promoting the resources and opportunities of Texas–specifically those in Tarrant County and the Birdville area. "It produces in ordinary seasons, in the most luxurant [sic] abundance, corn, wheat, rye, oats, barley millet, sorhgo cane [sorghum cultivated for syrup or fodder], cotton, potatoes, pumpkins, beans, peas, melons &c., &c., and that too but with little culture."[3] The writer believed that the elevated prairie lands were the best for agricultural purposes, but noted that "The river bottoms and valley lands are, too, very fertile—in fact extremely so, but as they would be, in a very

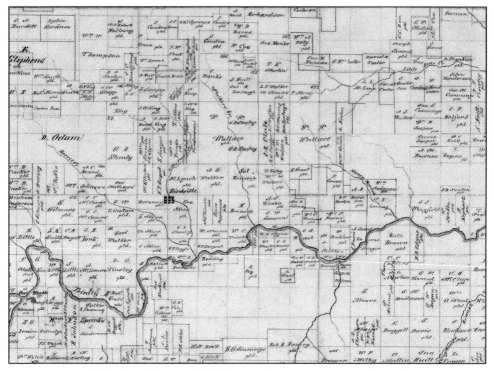

This detail from an 1856 Tarrant County survey map drawn by
F. H. Arlitt shows Birdville and, to the south, the area that would become
the Garden of Eden. Map 4068.
Courtesy Texas General Land Office, Austin.

wet time liable to overflow, they consequently are not so desirable for farming purposes."[4] While white farmers and ranchers sought the prairie lands, the bottomlands would provide an opportunity for Northeast Tarrant County's early African American residents—fertile land that was much more affordable than the more coveted prairie.

The town of Birdville was platted in 1851, shortly after the 1849 formation of Tarrant County, and served as the county seat from 1851 to 1856. George Akers donated eighty acres of land to secure the county seat designation. Lots were platted and sold to raise funds for the construction of a courthouse.[5] Although the area around Birdville thrived during the late 1840s and early 1850s, and many early settlers chose to establish their farms and ranches near the community, Birdville never overcame the gut-punch of the 1856 county seat election, often called the "whiskey-barrel election," because Fort Worth citizens freely used the libation to round up a handful of out-of-county voters and ensure that the county seat moved to Fort Worth. In 1870, Birdville had four businesses and a blacksmith shop.[6] Throughout the late nineteenth and early twentieth centuries, Birdville served as the small-town nucleus of a rural agricultural community where few people lived in town, but many went there to procure staples that they could not produce on their own (among these salt, pepper, sugar, textiles, ammunition, tobacco, liquor, and shoes). Today, Birdville no longer exists as a town, having been annexed by Haltom City in 1949, but the name survives in the Birdville Independent School District, a cemetery, several churches, and a historical society.[7]

Although African Americans had a difficult time during slavery and immediately following the Civil War, they did have white advocates in the Birdville area. Dr. Benjamin Franklin Barkley (1822-1882) and his wife Malinda (1827-1917) moved to Birdville in 1855, and he worked as both a physician and an attorney. The couple freed their slaves in Kentucky before moving to Texas and, once in Tarrant County, became the face of the miniscule abolitionist and anti-secessionist movements there.[8]

Following the Civil War, Barkley served as Tarrant County's Assistant Commissioner for the Bureau of Refugees, Freedmen, and Abandoned Lands from 1867 to 1868, and on the Tarrant County Registration Board, which handled voter eligibility and registration. As an advocate for free black suffrage, Barkley made it much easier for newly emancipated African American men to vote for the first time in their lives. His work with the Freedmen's Bureau was significant because he was the one person from whom former slaves could seek re-

Benjamin Franklin Barkley, who lived in Birdville, was a friend of freedmen in Tarrant County. Courtesy Tarrant County College NE, Heritage Room.

Opposite top: *The Barkley home also housed the Birdville post office, marked with a faint x on this photograph.* Opposite bottom: *Lon and Alice Barkley. Courtesy Tarrant County College NE, Heritage Room.*

dress when they were terrorized by Tarrant County's Ku Klux Klan. Under the Reconstruction government in place following the Civil War, Barkley served as county judge from 1867 to 1870 and as county treasurer between 1871 and 1873. Barkley was so frequently harassed, both in print and in public, for his actions furthering the rights of African Americans and the Reconstruction programs of the United States government that he had a contingent of African American soldiers accompany him whenever he made the trip from Birdville to Fort Worth.[9] Regardless of his political convictions, Barkley was a committed citizen. During the Civil War, he treated Confederate soldiers, assisted women who were widowed by the war, and served as a Confederate postmaster. Barkley also donated land for the Birdville Cemetery, where he, his wife, and their son Leonidas "Lon" Barkley are buried.

People who had neither worked for nor supported the Confederacy were in short supply in Tarrant County following the Civil War, so that the Barkley's fifteen-year-old daughter Francina Alice (called Alice by the family, but her first name may have helped fool government officials into thinking she was a man) was appointed postmistress in Birdville in 1866. She was reportedly the first postmistress in the United States.[10] Her brother Lon served as postmaster in Fort Worth from 1906 to 1908, and was referred to as the "cowboy postmaster" because he spent about eighteen years of his life working cattle on the Texas range.[11]

After the Civil War, African Americans from the Loyd and Boaz families established themselves in the river-bottom lands bordering the Trinity River and Little Fossil Creek, which provided water for cattle and agriculture. Underground springs were a source of water for drinking, and every household had hand-pumped water wells. The land, built up by the ebb and flow of flooding, consisted of sand, gravel, clay, and topsoil. Native trees, which still grow on the land, included pecan, cotonwood, elm, bois d'arc, willow, hackberry, post oak, and black walnut. Settlers planted fruit orchards, favoring plum, peach, and pear trees.

Limestone was hewn out of Little Fossil Creek to make fireplaces and chimneys.

Ed and Aurelia Boaz, who had been slaves of Samuel Boaz, located on land just west of Handley Ederville Road, bordered by Highway 121 and the Rock Island Railroad to the north, the Trinity River to the south, Big Fossil Creek to the east, and Minnis Drive to the west.

The Boazes had seven children: George, Clysta, Cunard, Copeland, Clara, Mary, and Sarah. (Ed's mother, Rachel Boaz, who lived next door, had a family of four: G. Boaz, G. W. Boaz, G. H. Boaz, and Jasper Boaz.) Sarah Boaz married Jimmy Johnson, and the couple lived for a time in the Garden of Eden area. Jimmy moved to follow work, taking farm jobs and other work where he could find it, so the Johnsons also lived in Corsicana and Dallas. After Jimmy Johnson's death, about 1910, Sarah Boaz Johnson moved back to Tarrant County to raise her two daughters, Edith and Lucinda.[12] Sarah raised her daughters alone until her death in 1916. Her will asked that her sister, Clara, and brother-in-law, Joe Wilson, take care of the girls until they were eighteen, so Edith and Lucinda lived on what is now Beach Street with Clara and Joe Wilson and their family.

Following the Civil War, Green and Charlotte Loyd lived next to Hale and Rebecca Loyd on what is now Elliott Reeder Road, north of the Trinity River. Their children included Henry, the oldest; Eliza; Julia; Malinda, who was born in Tarrant County and may have been named for Malinda Barkley; Emma; Lee; Martin, who may have been named for Martin B. Loyd; Ida; Dick; Abe; and Mary Ann. Hale Loyd, Green Loyd's former owner, died in December 1871.[13] It is very likely that Green Loyd and his sons continued to work the land owned by his former owner's widow, Rebecca Loyd. The family made good economic gains and every indication is that their relationship with the white Loyd family was cordial. In 1871, the property tax rolls first show Green Loyd as owning five horses.[14] Before machinery, horses and mules were es-

Edith, left, and Lucinda Johnson as young girls. Sanders family collection.

sential assets for both farming and cattle raising. They allowed family members to do work for others on better terms than if they simply provided their own human labor.

Rush Loyd, who was Green Loyd's younger brother, also played an important role in the family's success. He was born into slavery about 1855, when the white Loyd family, headed by Hale Loyd, was in Mississippi; he moved with the Loyds to Texas. At some point after the Civil War, Rush Loyd went to work for two brothers, Robert and Joseph Lewis, who worked as stock raisers. According to the 1870 census, he resided with these two white men in the Birdville area, living close to both Hale Loyd and Green Loyd.[15] During this heady time, the cattle business offered an incredible business opportunity as longhorns were rounded up and trailed north to packing plants. The skills he learned likely helped Rush Loyd to become the first member of the African American Loyd family to own land.

On February 28, 1874, Rush Loyd received from Robertson's Colony a 160-acre preemption grant of land that had been abandoned by a previous grantee. The terms of the grant required him to live on the land for three years and make improvements. The grant was patented in October 1877, giving him full title to the land.[16] This land, called the Rush Loyd Survey, lies west of what is now North Main Street along Cement Creek and a bit south of Loop I-820, just west of Meacham Field.[17] Rush Loyd also obtained an unidentified tract of land in December 1874 from Lucy and George Reed. Although the Tarrant County Courthouse burned in 1876, destroying county records, this acquisition was referenced when Rush and his wife sold some of the property in 1879.[18] Loyd also owned property in downtown Fort Worth in 1876, described as "part" of Block 119 or Block B7 of Fort Worth.[19] That block is on the west side of Main Street, between Ninth and what would be Tenth streets. The 1885 Sanborn Fire Insurance Map for Fort Worth shows the block filled with the Central Wagon Yard, the City Carriage and Wagon Stop, a grocery, and several dwellings.[20] Rush Loyd owned the downtown property for a number of years, selling lots from time to time until 1893, when the Chicago Rock Island and Texas Railway, which completed its line into Fort Worth that same year, acquired a substantial portion of the block.[21] That block currently holds the northwestern corner of the Fort Worth Convention Center. The following year, Rush Loyd bought sixty-five acres out of the S. Elliott and W. R. Reeder surveys for $2,275—land that is part of the Garden of Eden.[22] The 1895 Sam Street's Map of Tarrant County, Texas, shows Rush Loyd's home located on this property. His land holdings and business operations doubtless improved the family's economic circumstances, and probably helped provide job opportunities for the extended family and led to future land acquisitions.

When Rush Loyd was in his mid-twenties, he faced a situation that was at once all too common and still horrific. In the early morning darkness of September 4, 1879, a man crept into the open bedroom window of Mrs. Bowman's house, located on Jones between Fifth and Sixth streets, where she and her young son were sleeping.[23] He dragged the twenty-eight-year-old woman to an adjacent room and raped her, crushing her throat with his hand to keep her from screaming. As she tried to run toward her front door, the man shoved her aside, threatening to kill her if she "hollered," and made his exit. Mrs. Bowman, who was recovering from typhoid fever, collapsed on the front stoop. In the immediate aftermath of the attack, she and a neighbor, C. M. Bloodgood, said they believed the attacker was an African American drayman who had previously moved furniture from a house next door to Mrs. Bowman.

They described the man to policeman Walter P. Thomas, who was first on the scene, and the officer thought he recognized the man as Rush Loyd.[24] Thomas went immediately to Loyd's house and arrested him. Rush Loyd emphatically denied the rape allegation, indicating that he had several witnesses who would attest that he was at home

Rush Loyd was held in this Tarrant County Jail building after he was arrested for an alleged rape. Newspaper accounts report that Sheriff Joe Henderson and his deputies kept watch from the porch and windows while protecting Loyd from a lynch mob.
Courtesy DeGolyer Library, Southern Methodist University.

asleep at the time of the attack. Loyd pointed out that he had been raised by Captain M. B. Loyd and that he was married, with a family—but Officer Thomas thought the alleged perpetrator looked nervous and excited, so he took him to the county jail.[25]

The next day, a rumor surfaced that the victim had died. It proved false, but County Attorney William S. Pendleton decided to take no chances and escorted Rush Loyd to Mrs. Bowman's home so that he could get her statement and she could make an identification. Word leaked that Loyd was out of his jail cell, and a crowd of about seventy-five people gathered, trying to locate and seize him. Rush Loyd was safely returned to the county jail. After their failure, the group decided to meet at the baseball field that evening and plot a further course of action. Mayor Robert E. Beckham came to the site and addressed the crowd, urging moderation--speaking through a partially open gate, as the mob would not let him onto the grounds. The situation became more tense when another crowd gathered on Main Street—reportedly 250 strong, with many onlookers—and marched toward the jail. Marshal Sam Farmer and a man named John Morris spoke to the crowd, urging them to refrain from violence and promising them that justice would be served. By 1:00 a.m. the numbers had dwindled, but several members of the group who reportedly had consumed too much "courage water" continued to argue about what action should be taken. A crowd of about fifty men with a dozen guns ended up near the jail, where "Sheriff Henderson and his men are sitting on the porch and in the windows, arms in hand, and masters of the situation."[26]

A later account provides additional details about a scene that played out much differently than it would in many other southern communities, where the accused was broken out of jail and lynched before he could be tried. The 1904 account said that Sheriff Joe Henderson and his deputies, all ex-Confederate soldiers, stood in a line at a post on Belknap Street. Henderson called out to the crowd, saying, "Gentlemen, this is the dead line, and if you cross it the leaders will certainly be shot down."[27] The crowd dispersed, leaving Rush Loyd unharmed. A few days later, he was moved to the jail in Dallas.[28] Loyd was tried twice. The first trial, held in March of 1880, resulted in a mistrial.[29] Reportedly, R. H. Tucker was the only member of the jury who voted for acquittal. Loyd was tried again in October of 1880 and found not guilty. By that time, another man named Isham Capps had allegedly confessed to the crime and been hanged.[30]

CHAPTER 4

Aunt Doll and the Sam Bass Stories:
Major Cheney Comes of Age

Dollie Cheney, Major and Malinda Cheney's youngest daughter, was born on October 25, 1887. She had long black hair and was heavyset. Her size gave her an imposing presence that filled the room. Aunt Doll, as everyone called her (she had no children of her own), was a fighter. She did not suffer fools gladly, and her mind was like a flypaper trap. As she was growing up, Major Cheney told his daughter stories about his childhood and young adult life in Tarrant County, and she became the repository for the family's history.

Dollie Cheney outlived her parents and all of her siblings by a substantial period of time. She did not hesitate to communicate her opinions or her stories, well aware that if she wanted younger generations to remember her parents' legacy, frequent repetition of her stories was necessary. Her stories don't exist in any official written record, but there is no doubt on the part of anyone in the Cheney family that Aunt Doll knew exactly what she was talking about. If not *completely* true, they are undoubtedly *mostly* true, and these stories instilled a strong sense of family pride in every relative who heard them. Thus, if Dollie Cheney's story of Major Cheney's friendship with Sam Bass isn't completely true, it should have been!

The records do not indicate when Major Cheney left Lavaca County, but his white half-brother, John G. Cheney, and John's wife Eliza moved to the Birdville area during the late 1870s. Family oral history says that Major Cheney came with the couple when they moved to Tarrant County and that he lived with them for a number of years, but Major may have left Lavaca County earlier. In December 1879, John G. Cheney paid $4,000 for 246 acres of Tarrant County land purchased from Manerva and John Boone "on the waters of the west fork of [the] Trinity river" in the John Akers, Thomas Akers, and John Walker surveys.[1] This land was on the western edge of the area that would become the Garden of Eden. The Cheney family ended up on land between the Boazes' and Loyds' holdings, so Major had the opportunity to become friends with them. Working the Cheneys' land enabled Major Cheney to learn farming and blacksmithing, and how to raise cows and horses. This part of Tarrant County was only four miles east of downtown Fort Worth and one and one-half to two miles south of Birdville. Most African Americans referred to this area as Birdville; whites called it Lower Birdville. Major Cheney referred to it as the Garden of Eden, and it is where many of his descendants still live today.

While living in Birdville, Major Cheney met a very interesting fellow. Birdville was only thirty miles south of Denton, where a man named Sam Bass was living. Sam Bass was born on a farm in Lawrence County, Indiana, on July 21, 1851. His mother died when he was ten years old, and Sam lived with his father and his father's new wife as well as with his uncle before deciding, in 1869, to move out on his own. He had heard of the Reno brothers, who were train robbers, and stories about them fascinated him to the point that he wanted to be a train robber himself. Sam left home and went to St. Louis, then decided to take a boat down the Mississippi River as far as he could afford to go. He got off at Rosedale, Mississippi, where he worked for a year. While working, he met a family that was going to Denton, Texas, and Sam decided to go there, too.

Sam fell in love with the town of Denton and with horses, so much so that he started racing them throughout North Texas. He began to

Sam Bass returned to Texas in 1878 from a series of bank and train robberies in the Midwest and continued his exploits. He is standing at the back left in this photograph, the only authenticated image of Bass.
Courtesy of True West *magazine archives.*

gamble on the horses, a lifestyle that can quickly empty your coffers if you aren't careful. Feeling that he needed fast money, Sam and a group of unsavory friends decided to rob banks, stagecoaches, and trains. Sam was not successful in this trade either, but he robbed enough stages to keep the gang happy.

Sam Bass was already deeply engaged in his trade when he met Major Cheney. Birdville was a shortcut to a lot of Sam's favorite haunts, and he made frequent rest stops there. Major, who was just five years younger than Bass, was an excellent horseman and could ride with the best of them. He owned horses and frequently swapped them out with Sam. Not only would Major take care of Sam's horses, he would let the gang stay at his place. Sam would feed his horses, trade out lame ones for new stock, and find himself a good meal. This part of Birdville was called the "bottom" because it was adjacent to the Trinity River. There were many trails leading in all directions and, in the summer, there were many places on the Trinity River that could be forded on horseback. No one knows how many years Major rode with Sam, but according to Dollie Cheney, it wasn't long. She thinks the main thing Major did for Sam was take care of the horses and give him a place to stay.

One of Sam's biggest robberies took place in Big Springs, Nebraska, in 1877. He and his gang robbed a train carrying $60,000 in twenty-dollar gold pieces. There were so many coins the horses couldn't carry them all, so Sam told his men to split up the gold. Two of them rode off to the southeast, and two of them rode off to Kansas City. Sam, with a friend, bought an old wagon and a two-bit horse and rode back to Texas. They hid the gold coins in the bottom of the wagon and dressed themselves to look like common folk. They were stopped only once by soldiers who were looking for the robbers, but were not arrested.

When Sam and his gang got back to Texas, he paid for goods and services from his stash of double-eagle coins. These coins were distributed within a hundred-mile radius of Denton, and Major likely received more than a few of them. Dollie Cheney told a story of seeing twenty-dollar gold pieces lying around on the floor. The children in the house would play with the money, and Dollie would holler at them saying, "Leave my Daddy's coins alone."

Major reportedly rode with Sam Bass on his last bank robbery attempt in Round Rock, Texas. A man who wanted other charges against him dropped agreed to alert the Texas Rangers about the planned holdup, and joined the gang under a ruse. On the morning of July 19,

1878, before Sam could get into the bank, the Rangers shot Sam and killed several members of his gang. Sam was put on his horse, bleeding, and led to a place right outside of town. He asked an African American woman to shelter him while he recovered, but she refused, so Sam lay down in the grass under a live oak tree. When Sam was spotted by the sheriff and his men, they didn't initially believe he was the infamous Sam Bass. Sam admitted he was the bank robber, but wouldn't give up the names of his gang members.[2] Sam Bass died at 3:58 p.m. on Sunday, July 21, 1878, his twenty-seventh birthday.[3]

Major Cheney was with Sam that day, according to Dollie Cheney, but was able to escape. What happened next was doubtless more hair-raising than the flight from the law. Major ran so far out on the plains between Round Rock and Georgetown that he was captured by Indians, who sewed him up in buffalo hide and left him to die. A white family traveling in a covered wagon saw the hide and noticed something struggling, trying to get out. They got out of their wagon, cut through the hide, and found a frantic Major inside. After they helped him out, Major told them the story of being captured, sewn up, and left to die. The white family was headed toward Birdville, so Major returned home with them.

Major began to settle down for good—there would be no more wild adventures with bank robbers. He was twenty-two years old in 1878 and had met a beautiful young lady by the name of Malinda Loyd, the daughter of Green and Charlotte Loyd. She was six years younger than Major, but he knew that she was the girl he was going to marry. Green Loyd was a prosperous farmer at this point, owning both horses and mules, and was able to make a good living for his family. Major Cheney could work with horses, had good farming skills, and maintained a valuable friendship with his white half-brother, John G. Cheney. Major Cheney and Malinda Loyd were married on August 31, 1881, in Tarrant County. Major was twenty-five and Malinda was nineteen years old.

CHAPTER 5

Early Life in the Garden of Eden

As the 1880s dawned and Major and Malinda Cheney began their life together in the Garden of Eden, a number of changes affected them. John G. Cheney died of typhoid fever in January 1880, leaving his wife Eliza a widow only six months after the family had bought land in Tarrant County.[1] Eliza J. Cheney then had five people living with her, including her son, John O. Cheney, who was twenty-one, his wife Trina, their one-year old son John, and Eliza's own younger daughters named Catherine and Alzada.[2] Major Cheney undoubtedly missed the support and friendship of John G. Cheney, who had known him his whole life.

During this time Jim Crow legislation began to extend its long arms, formalizing segregation that had previously been informal or left to the discretion of the parties involved. Although laws had regulated relationships between whites and African Americans (both slave and free), giving few, if any, rights to slaves, the fact that both races lived on the same farm or plantation meant that the two groups had fairly regular interaction.[3] That began to change after the demise of the plantation system. When Republican Reconstructionists pulled out of Texas in 1874, laws were created that more strictly regulated interactions between the races—regulations that covered everything from marriage to railroad travel.

After slavery ended, both African American and white branches of the Boaz and Loyd families lived near each other on land that collectively came to be called the Garden of Eden, so named for its fertile soil and the generally peaceful existence the river bend location offered. John G. Cheney had bought land in the same area, and Major Cheney likely lived with or near the family until he and Malinda Loyd married and acquired land of their own. The 1882 Tarrant County tax rolls, which listed and valued property for taxation purposes, showed that although Major Cheney owned no land, he did own two horses valued at $12.50 each and two head of cattle valued at $10 each.[4] He may have been helping Eliza Cheney and her son, John O. Cheney, farm their land, but he was also likely assisting Green Loyd and Rush Loyd with their farmwork.

In June of 1885 Major and Malinda had their first child, whom they named Hattie. Mary was the second daughter, born in August of 1886. She was nice looking, short and slightly pudgy, with long, sandy hair. In October 1887, a third daughter named Dollie joined the family. These three girls were very close—wherever you saw one, the other two were always close by. Their closest friends were Lillie and Hattie Hooper, who lived in Riverside, a black community three miles west of Birdville, where Malinda's father, Green Loyd, also lived. These girls went to church and school together. Major and Malinda's first son, Lon, was born in January of 1890.

Major bought his first acreage in the Garden of Eden in 1887, from a white friend named Landon Booth, a prominent landowner in Tarrant County.[5] He continued to acquire land, eventually ending up with over two hundred acres.[6] Although the land in the Trinity River bottoms that Major Cheney farmed was very fertile, it was not in high demand because of the potential for flooding. It was, in many ways, the perfect place—productive, but set aside from the more desirable land preferred by whites. It was a place to build a family and a good life. Major Cheney farmed, growing corn, greens, peas, tomatoes, grapes, peaches, pears, plums, watermelons, and pecans. They used water from the Trinity River to irrigate crops and water their cattle.

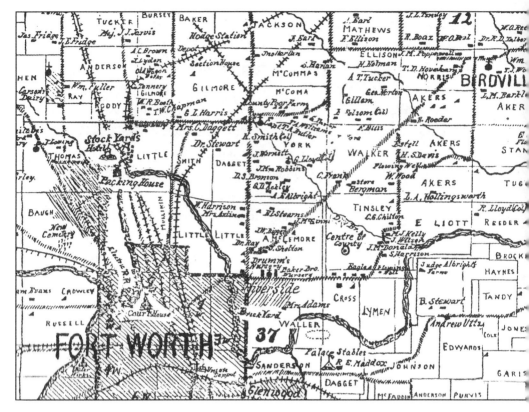

This detail from Sam Street's 1895 map of Tarrant County shows the area around Birdville with homeowners marked with a rectangle and renters or tenants marked with a triangle. Both Rush Loyd and Major Cheney owned land in the Garden of Eden at this time, but only Loyd is shown as a homeowner. Hodge Station, where the Cheney family took their cattle to market, is in the upper left corner. Public domain image.

In the late 1880s or early 1890s, Major built a home two miles east of Carson Street, on what is now Elliott Reeder Road, to house his growing family. The house, which lay about three-quarters of a mile north of the Trinity River, was a substantial wood-frame structure.[7] North Texas farmhouses built during this time were not the high-style Victorian era homes constructed for city residents, but functional houses built according to traditional plans. They are often referred to today as "folk"

Major Cheney about 1910.
Sanders family collection.

houses. The Cheney's home was a one-story, T-shaped building with a front porch, similar to the houses built by neighboring farm owners. For an African American family of that period, it was a grand and impressive residence.

Farm life revolved around schedules, both at home and in the fields. Major Cheney was in charge of the farming and cattle operations, while Malinda Cheney ran the household. The family used all of the land that could be planted to grow crops. Major Cheney planted crops that required the most intensive cultivation in an area called "the meadow." He used a one- or two-mule (sometimes horse-drawn) plow to prepare the ground and always planted his crops on Good Friday. Corn was a major crop, but Major also grew okra, black-eyed peas, and other beans. The black-eyed pea plants were planted among the corn stalks to hide them from animals and thieves. The family used corn to make hominy, ground it for cornmeal, and canned it for winter eating. The cows ate the silage, and some corn was left out to dry and then shocked—that is, the stalk was cut and gathered with other stalks into bundles that stood with the butt end on the ground. The shocks were used to feed the cattle and hogs. There was also an area on the farm where sweet potatoes were grown. The truckloads of sweet potatoes were covered in a kiln under a layer of hay and dirt to keep them cool.

Cattle grazed in a grassy area in the river bottom that had a lot of trees. The trees made the land difficult to plow, so it was better suited for grazing. The family did grow a small amount of corn as well as Johnson grass in the river bottoms, both used to feed livestock. The family's horses, mules, pigs, milk cows, and beef cattle lived behind the main house in a barn and in lots around the barn that were fenced off from the back yard. The barn had cribs, stalls, feed racks, troughs, and storage for harnesses. The cattle were taken out each morning to graze and brought back to the cow lot at night.

One portion of tree-laden Trinity River bottomland served as the Cheneys' woodlot. Post oak trees were cut in the woodlot, hauled back to the house, and split, using a log-splitting wedge and a single-blade axe. Children picked up small fallen branches for kindling. The Cheney children were also involved in gathering pecans from the native trees that grew near the Trinity. Everyone in the family had their own tree and was allowed to keep the money he or she made from gathering and selling the pecans from "their" tree. Dollie Cheney planted a num-

Family members pose with a reaper, used to gather hay in the fields.
The back of Major and Malinda Cheney's home is visible in the background.
This is the only known photograph of their residence, which burned in 1946.
Sanders family collection.

ber of papershell pecan trees, and those nuts were kept for family use.

The agricultural fields were fenced with barbed wire, which required a lot of upkeep. Any spare time left after planting, tending, or harvesting crops was likely occupied by fence repairs. Fence posts were cut from the few cedar and bois d'arc trees that grew on the farm property.

Major Cheney specialized in growing watermelons in the rich, sandy, bottomland soil near the river. Some of them weighed more than fifty pounds. The crops were harvested in September, and sometimes the male children had to miss school in order to help with the harvest. Major hauled his crops to the courthouse square in Fort Worth using mules and a wagon. He always made a hefty profit on his crops, especially the watermelons. After selling everything he had hauled into town that day, Major would stop off at the White Elephant Saloon for a drink. Sometimes he would drink a bit too much. Friends and tavern owners would put him in his wagon, and his team of mules would bring him home. When the wagon and team got to the house, Malinda would hear them. She would go out to the wagon, lift him out, and carry him into the house.

Because Major Cheney farmed almost two hundred acres, he hired workers from surrounding towns to help him work the land, and he provided housing for some of them. When the Cheney children grew up and married, they also needed places to live, so during the early twentieth century, a number of small homes were constructed near the main house on the farm property, making the Cheney farm a true community.

Malinda Cheney was the matriarch of that community. She presided over the main house, and her reach extended to the back yard, including the garden, orchard, and berry patches. Malinda's domain was impressive. As visitors approached the house from the road, they passed a red picket fence and entered a walkway dividing a yard that was bordered by flowers. The house had a general T-shaped plan, with the top of the T facing the main road. Steps led to the front porch, which had a swing hanging from the ceiling that provided a favorite place to sit during the warmer months. Rosebushes ran along the front of the house, and four entrances provided access from the front porch. The central entrance led into a bedroom that also had a sleeping porch on its east side, with three beds. Screened sleeping porches provided a

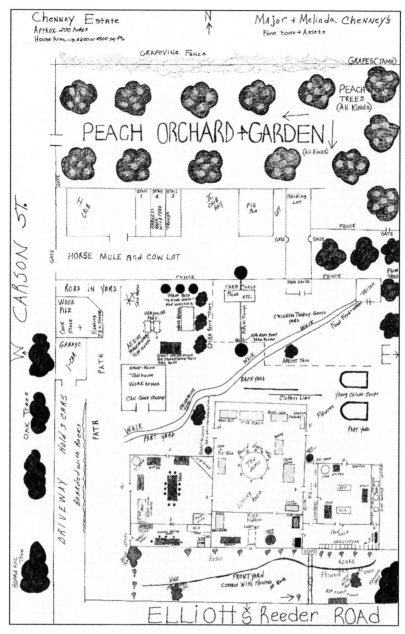

A. J. "Buddy" Sanders, who was Major and Malinda's great-grandson, drew this plot plan showing the layout of the main house, yard, and garden area. It shows the setting after 1924, when the house was moved from its original location to accommodate sand and gravel mining. Sanders family collection.

cooler place to rest during the hot summer months before air conditioning cooled houses. The sleeping porch was protected by awnings that could be raised or lowered as the angle of the sun dictated.

Another entrance from the front porch led west into the main bedroom. The main bedroom was very large. It contained a large bed, wardrobe, dresser, cedar chest, lamp table, and another chest. The rosebushes along the front of the house were visible through a central window. This was where Major and Malinda slept, often with their newest baby nearby.

A doorway led from the main bedroom into the living room, which was the largest room in the house. The living room had a linen closet, a cake and pie table (to hold all of Malinda's excellent desserts), a woodbox, a fireplace, a book table, a sewing machine, a buffet, and a large round dining table with ten chairs. During the cooler months of fall, winter, and spring, this room was the center of family life, where meals were eaten and visitors entertained. The noise level was probably loud at times, especially when friends and their families came for Sunday dinner, and neighborhood gossip as well as discussion of family and political matters filled the air.

The kitchen, off the living room to the west, held a large dinner and breakfast table that seated ten people. There was also an icebox that could store one hundred pounds of ice, a water table or sink, a woodstove with its attendant woodbox, a cupboard, and a pantry that Malinda Cheney called her "grocery store." The icebox and woodstove were necessary because the house was built before electricity was a common convenience. That meant that you had to haul blocks of ice to keep perishable food cool—especially during the hot summer months—and needed a ready supply of wood, split and chopped to the proper size, to keep the woodstove at the proper temperature for cooking or baking. Preparing meals for a large family was almost a full-time occupation.

There were no pre-prepared foods, and most of the meat, vegetables, and fruits came directly from the family's garden or farming operations.

The second screened-in porch was used mainly for dining in the summertime. In this room, there was a place for a second water table or sink, a milk table used to store jugs of milk produced by the family's cows, and yet another dining table with chairs for ten people. This room could also serve as an auxiliary food preparation area when meals were being prepared for a crowd.

In contrast to the front yard filled with flowers, the back yard was bare dirt that had to be swept clean on a regular basis. The back yard held water barrels for storing rainwater, which lessened the reliance on well water and was good for washing clothes. There was also a clothes-line, a wide variety of coops for all types of poultry, including chickens, turkeys, and the always-reliable burglar alarm—geese, who announced any arrival with a chorus of honking. The poultry was fenced in, supplied with water and feed troughs. There was also a shed in which poultry feed was stored. Major had a smokehouse, tool house, workbench, and a giant grinding stone used to sharpen axes and other tools. Malinda also had a place to store the canned goods she and her daughters produced using the farm's fruits and vegetables.

The back yard also had huge cast-iron wash pots that were used to heat water and wash clothes, a wash bench where stains and dirt were scrubbed out, and a clothesline where the family's garments were hung to dry. Water was supplied from a well, using a hand pump and draw bucket.

Beyond the barn were peach, pear, and plum orchards with different varieties of the various fruits that were eaten fresh, canned, or made into jams and jellies. The back line of the farm to the north was defined by a fence where mustang grapes grew in the same place every year. The native grapes were used to make jelly and wine. To the east of the

*The Cheney-Sanders family shares a long tradition of bountiful Sunday
dinners, and treasured family recipes are often on the table.
Hasson Diggs, photographer.*

house were more gardens.

Last, but not least, at the far back corner of the yard, was a two-seater
outhouse, which you had to walk through the poultry yard to reach.

Major Cheney had a place in back of the house to park his three
wagons, one for hauling produce and materials, a hack, and a carriage.
He also had storage space for all of his plows. Mr. and Mrs. Joe Woods,
of Mosier Valley, said that in the early 1920s Malinda and Major would
come to Mosier Valley to visit, riding in their hack with A. J. "Buddy"
Sanders, their toddler great-grandson, standing up between them. In
the late 1920s, Malinda Cheney built a driveway and a garage on the
west side of the property that was one car wide but long enough to hold

three cars. The driveway was bordered with rocks and oak trees. The garage would later become a room for boarders. It had a woodstove, woodbox, and a heating fireplace.

Malinda Cheney reserved one particular spot of the farm for herself, about a two-acre plot where she would plant a crop of cotton. This was the only place on the farm where cotton was grown. The money she made from it would be used to buy Christmas gifts for family and friends. Picking cotton by hand was backbreaking work, but Malinda did it, because every boll she pulled meant a bit of extra money that she could use to honor people she loved.

Malinda learned to cook at an early age, and she could cook anything. Her specialties were blackbird pie and pecan pound cake. She cooked the daily meals, but family celebrations and festivities with special foods, including the tradition of bountiful Sunday dinners for family and friends, began when the Garden of Eden was very young. It is a tradition that continues to this day, and recipes beloved by other family members were added to the menu over the years. A number of Malinda's recipes survive and are still used by family members. Sunday dinner featured tables loaded with all manner of food and drink, and it wasn't unusual for all of the house's tables to be full of appreciative diners.

Among the favorite recipes that Malinda and other family members prepared for those bountiful dinners include:

Old-Fashioned Chicken and Dumplings

Chicken:
1 chicken
1-1/2 tablespoons water
1 tablespoon flour
Dumplings:

2 cups flour
1 teaspoon salt
2 teaspoons baking powder
1/3 cup shortening
sweet milk*

Stew chicken in water to cover until meat falls from the bones. Remove bones from the stock and discard. Set meat aside. Mix flour and water into a fine paste; add to stock.

Dumplings: Sift together the flour, baking powder, and salt; cut in shortening, and add enough sweet milk to make a soft dough. Let the dough stand awhile. Roll out thinly and cut into squares. Meanwhile, bring prepared chicken stock to a boil. Add chicken, then drop squares into stock. Drop in layers and allow broth to boil over each layer before adding another. Cover and cook for 12-15 minutes. Serve with cornbread and tossed salad.

that is, not buttermilk, but homogenized whole milk

Mama 'Nez's Meat Loaf

3 pounds ground beef
1 medium onion
2 eggs
¼ cup ketchup
1 small green bell pepper, chopped
1 stalk celery, chopped
1 sleeve saltine crackers, crushed
dash of cayenne pepper
dash of curry powder
salt and pepper to taste

flour

2 (8-ounce) cans tomato sauce

1 (8-ounce) can water

In a large bowl combine ground beef, onion, eggs, ketchup, one can tomato sauce, green bell pepper, celery, crackers, curry powder, cayenne pepper, salt and pepper; mix well. Add more crackers if needed to form the perfect loaf. Mold and shape into a loaf, making sure there are no cracks. Sprinkle a little flour over the top. Pour the remaining can of tomato sauce over the loaf, followed by one can of water. Cook in oven at 325° until done.

Chitlins* and Hog Maws

5 pounds hog maws,** thoroughly cleaned, cut in squares and excess fat trimmed

2 pounds chitlins, thoroughly cleaned

1 large onion, chopped

2 stalks celery, chopped

salt to taste

pepper to taste

dash of curry

dash of red pepper

½ cup white vinegar

1 medium potato, scrubbed

1 jalapeño pepper

Place hog maws and chitlins in a large stock pot. Cover with water. Be sure the hog maws are on the bottom. Add onion, celery, salt, black pepper, curry, and red pepper. Add ½ cup white vinegar, one medium potato, and one jalapeño pepper. Cover and bring to a boil. Reduce heat and cook over medium heat until tender (approximately 3 to 4 hours). Remove the potato when chitlins are done. The potato helps to absorb the aroma. Serve chitlins and hog maws with greens and cornbread.

Variations: Chitlins may also be sautéed in bacon drippings or in hot oil. Another alternative is to dip the cooked chitlins into beaten egg batter, roll in cracker meal, and deep fry at 385° in hot fat until golden brown. Drain on paper towel and serve hot! Any other leftovers may be placed in foil with barbecue sauce poured on top and grilled until desired flavor or texture is reached.

*chitterlings

**Also called pork maws, these are available at Fiesta super-markets and at markets serving African American communities.

Fried Chicken

Note: *This recipe was altered at some point to include garlic salt and pancake mix. The older version likely called for minced garlic, regular table salt, and flour.*

1 fryer, cut up, washed, and patted dry
black pepper
red pepper
garlic salt
1½ cups vegetable oil
Batter:
½ cup pancake mix
1-1/2 cups water

Flour Mixture:
2 cups flour
2 tablespoons baking powder
black pepper
red pepper
garlic salt

Mix together batter ingredients (not too thin). Season chicken with black pepper, red pepper, and garlic salt. In a large skillet heat the oil over medium heat until a drop of water sizzles in it. Dip chicken pieces in batter and then into the flour mixture. Place chicken in skillet and cook over medium heat until golden brown. Turn the pieces occasionally while cooking, so that chicken is crisp on the outside and the insides are fully cooked. Don't brown too quickly. Use enough oil to come midway up the chicken pieces when placed in the skillet.

Mama Edith's Baked Sweet Potatoes

10 medium sweet potatoes
butter
Wash sweet potatoes thoroughly. Pat dry with a paper towel. With pastry brush, grease potatoes all over with butter. Place on ungreased cookie sheet and bake in oven at 450° until potatoes are easily pierced with a fork.

Aunt Cindy's Candied Yams

4 medium sweet potatoes or yams, peeled and sliced into rounds about ½ inch thick

3 cups water
4 tablespoons butter
½ cup sugar
¼ teaspoon vanilla flavoring
cinnamon (optional)
brown sugar (optional)
nutmeg (optional)

Place potatoes in a large saucepan. Fill pan with three cups of water. Cook potatoes over medium heat until they come to a boil. Pour off water. Place potatoes in a glass baking dish. Dot with butter. Sprinkle sugar and vanilla over potatoes; add spices as desired. Bake at 400° until tender.

Mama 'Nez's Hot Water Cornbread

hot water
1 tablespoon salt
2 cups white cornmeal
1 tablespoon Crisco Butter Flavor Shortening*
oil for frying

Bring the water to a rolling boil. The trick is in the water; it must be boiling hot. Mix cornmeal, salt, and shortening in a large bowl. Stir in just enough boiling water to make a soft dough. Shape into pones and fry in a single layer until golden brown on both sides, turning once. Makes approximately 12 pones. After you've finished cooking the pones, split them open and butter immediately. Best served with greens and navy or pinto beans.

the original recipe called for lard

Malinda Cheney's Pecan Pound Cake

This is one of the earliest versions of the Cheney family's celebrated "1-2-3-4" cakes, so-called because each one uses 1 cup of butter, 2 cups of sugar, 3 cups of flour, and 4 eggs. There were a number of recipes developed over the years using this tried-and-true formula. It was the most-requested recipe in the 2005 Fort Worth Star-Telegram's *"Reader Recipe Swap."*[8]

1 cup butter
2 cups sugar
4 eggs
3 cups flour
1 tablespoon baking powder
1 cup milk
1 tablespoon vanilla
1 cup pecans, chopped

In a large bowl, cream butter and sugar until light and fluffy, beating for several minutes. Add eggs one at a time, beating well after each addition. Sift flour three times, measuring each time. On the final sifting, sift the baking powder into the third cup. Spoon flour into the butter mixture a little at a time, adding a little milk each time. After the mixture is well blended, add vanilla. After all ingredients are blended well, sprinkle a small amount of flour over the pecans and fold into the batter. Grease and flour two 4" x 8" loaf pans. Pour batter into the loaf pans and bake at 325° for 1 hour or until a toothpick inserted into the center comes out clean. Do not preheat oven!

Malinda Cheney's Tea Cakes

2 sticks butter
2 cups sugar
2 eggs
4 cups flour
1 level teaspoon nutmeg
1 level teaspoon baking soda
1 cup buttermilk
1 teaspoon vanilla

Have all ingredients at room temperature for best results. In a large mixing bowl combine butter and sugar; beat until smooth and creamy. Add eggs one at a time and beat until fluffy. Sift or stir together the flour, nutmeg, and baking soda; add the dry ingredients to the egg mixture about a cup at a time, beating after each addition. Add vanilla and buttermilk and stir until blended. Spoon or drop cookie dough onto cookie sheet and bake at 400° until lightly browned.

Tip: The original recipe calls for all mixing or beating to be done by hand; however an electric mixer may be used if desired.

Opposite: *Robert Johnson Jr. (the son of Robert and Dilsie Johnson) with his wife Sallie and their daughter Delilah about 1890, outside their home in Mosier Valley.*
Courtesy Tarrant County College NE, Heritage Room.

CHAPTER 6

Other African American Communities in Tarrant County and How They Relate to the Garden of Eden

By the 1880s, African Americans in Tarrant County had begun to acquire property and define their own communities. In addition to the Garden of Eden, there were other substantial African American enclaves in east and northeast Tarrant County, including Mosier Valley, Stop Six, Riverside, Hodge Station, Dove, and Grapevine. Several of them had significant connections to the Garden of Eden.

Opal Trigg Woods, standing third from right, at a cake baking competition in Mosier Valley during the 1950s. Sanders family collection.

Mosier Valley

The earliest freedmen's community in Tarrant County, Mosier Valley was established in the early 1870s when plantation owner Lucy Lee gave a tract of land as a wedding gift to her former slaves, Robert and Dilsie Johnson, and ten other slave families purchased adjacent tracts of Trinity River bottomland.[1] The community is located on the north side of the Trinity, southwest of Euless and the Dallas/Fort Worth International Airport. Much like the Garden of Eden, the families farmed, keeping livestock, growing cash crops like cotton and corn for sale, and raising vegetables for themselves. Mosier Valley had a Baptist church and a school, established in 1883, and, at its height between 1910 and 1930, a population of about three hundred. Geographically, it was the closest African American community to the Garden of Eden, so families like the Parkers, Woodses, Sheltons, and Morses would have had frequent business and social interactions with the black families living near Birdville. Inez Trigg Sanders and Gladys Trigg Sanders had an older sister named Opal who married Joe Woods, a descendant of an important Mosier Valley family. The couple spent a great deal of time in the Garden of Eden because her sisters lived there, and eventually Joe and Opal built a home there as well. Fort Worth annexed Mosier Valley in 1960, as Dallas and Fort Worth were considering the construction of the Dallas/Fort Worth airport.

Stop Six

Stop Six received its name because it was the sixth and final Fort Worth stop on the Interurban before the train headed on to Dallas.[2] Amanda Robins Davis, who spent most of her life in Stop Six, was born April 1, 1866, to Ben Robins and his wife, Ann.[3] Growing up, she lived with her mother and stepfather, Frank Brockman, on the old Hall place, in what is now the Polytechnic area of Fort Worth. Amanda married Mack Davis in the mid-1880s. In 1896, she paid forty-five dollars for a one-acre tract of land east of Polytechnic and became one of the first African American property owners in the area. Amanda lived to be ninety-four years old, and she recounted many tales of early life in the area. She talked about how her family would trade with the Indians, giving them meat in exchange for blankets. Alonzo and Sarah Cowan, a black couple, bought land nearby in 1902, and the area became known as Cowanville. The name Stop Six gradually supplanted the old name, probably because it was shorter and easier to remember.

The street Amanda lived on was later named "Amanda Street," for her. She became a stalwart in the neighborhood and was affiliated with two churches, Mayfield Baptist Church and Ebenezer Baptist Church. Both church buildings were within walking distance of her house.

Amanda Davis was an early resident of the Stop Six neighborhood. Her eldest son, Jimmy Sanders, married Hattie Cheney, Major and Malinda Cheney's eldest daughter, establishing ties between the two families.
Sanders family collection.

Mack and Amanda Davis had eight children together (Julius, Annie, Mack Jr., Winnie, Mollie, Katie Bell, Warren, and Bennie), but Amanda had two children before she married Mack.[4] Amanda Davis and her older daughters worked as washerwomen. Jimmy Sanders, Amanda's firstborn, was born in 1883 and was, reportedly, fathered by a white doctor who lived in Fort Worth. When Dr. Sanders's relatives found out that he had fathered a black child, they wouldn't have anything to do with him, and he was told to leave Fort Worth.

Julius Davis, Amanda's eldest son with Mack, worked for the Texas and Pacific Railway. Julius was a World War I veteran and played a twelve-string guitar with a band that traveled Europe during the 1920s. He confirmed the story about Jimmy Sanders, who was reportedly light-skinned, tall, and very athletic. Jimmy Sanders provides the Sanders family connection to the Garden of Eden, as he married Hattie Cheney, Major and Malinda's oldest daughter, in 1901.[5] He died in 1902 of internal injuries sustained when he lifted a handcar off the railroad tracks to avoid a collision with a train.

Jessie Howard was Amanda Davis's other son born prior to her marriage with Mack. Like his half brothers Jimmy Sanders and Julius Davis, he worked for the Texas and Pacific Railway. Frank Howard, Jessie's son and Amanda's grandson, loved growing up in the rural area and shared memories of it, much as his grandmother liked to do. He hunted rabbits on the open lands between Fort Worth and Arlington and fished in Village Creek. Frank pastored the St. Paul Reformed Baptist Church, worked as a musical instrument repairman, and married a singer, Senola Felder, in 1933. The couple lived in Stop Six for the remainder of their lives.[6]

Amanda's daughter Annie Davis had a daughter named Johnnie B. Bell who had a special gift of prophecy. Although she was an invalid and confined to bed for over fifty years, Johnnie B. told fortunes to make a living. She believed that her ability to predict the future came from

Ida Loyd, Malinda Cheney's sister, married George McClardy Sr.
This photograph shows the family about 1910. Front row: Ida Loyd
McClardy, Nicholas, George McClardy Sr. Back row: Samantha, Manda,
Spencer, Minnie, and George Jr. Thyssen family collection.

God and that she could use her insight to assist people and help them
lead better lives.[7]

Riverside and Hodge Station

In 1885, Green Loyd purchased ten acres of land in the Riverside
area, near present-day Carter Riverside High School, making him one
of the first African American settlers in that area. Hodge Station was on
the northern boundary of Riverside, near the Colorado and Southern
Railroad, where cattle were loaded and unloaded. It was an adjunct site

Hodge Station was a rail junction first used to load and unload cattle. Railroad services and industrial uses followed, and many who worked there lived nearby. This 1976 view shows rail cars through the broken windows of an abandoned railroad bunk house.
Courtesy Fort Worth Star-Telegram *Collection. Special Collections, the University of Texas at Arlington Library, Arlington, Texas.*

Corinth Baptist Church, located at 2700 Ennis Avenue in Riverside, was the Cheneys' church home for many years prior to the construction of Valley Baptist Church. Courtesy Fort Worth Star-Telegram Collection. Special Collections, The University of Texas at Arlington Library, Arlington, Texas.

for handling livestock a short distance from the Fort Worth Stockyards.

People from Riverside would find their way to the Cheney farm, often for overnight stays. In the summertime the Riverside folks would come out to fish and get vegetables. During the fall and winter months, they would fish, hunt, and barbecue. In addition to the Loyds, who were already related because Malinda was married to Major Cheney, the Cox, Finnel, Guerry, Hooper, McClardy, and Ross families were among the Riverside households that made visits to the Garden of Eden. Burton and Lottie Guerry had seven children (Jimmy, John, Almen, Florence, Nathan, Josie, and Ethel). Their son John married Mary Cheney, and

Ida Loyd married George McClardy in 1892, cementing relationships among the families. George and Ida McClardy cared for Green Loyd during his later years, in their home on Beach Street.

As the family and the community around them grew, so did the institutions that supported a richer life. Corinth Baptist Church was organized in the spring of 1886, an offshoot of Mount Gilead Baptist Church in downtown Fort Worth. The church was located in Hodge Station, near what is now the intersection of 28th Street and Sylvania Avenue.[8] The first church meeting was held in the school building in that community. Soon, the church purchased a lot for $50 from Harrison Thompson for the first church site and built a one-room building where they worshipped for six years.

Charter members of Corinth Baptist included Harrison and Delia Thompson and family, the Guerrys, Major and Malinda Cheney, Green and Charlotte Loyd, Jim Davis, George Brazer, Bill Mathes, Elie Louder, Lillie McKee, Carolina Copeland, Amie Bell, Rosa Davis, Tennessee Fenley, and Susan Matthews. Reverend John Bell served as the first pastor, assisted by Reverend Brooks, and Reverend C. P. Hughes, of Mount Gilead Baptist Church, helped establish the church.

As Riverside began to grow and the blacks in Hodge Station began to sell their land, the church members decided to seek a new location. They agreed to move south to Riverside. Gid Hooper was a deacon of the church. He asked Judge Booth, a real estate man, for land to hold a school and church in the Riverside area. The old one-room frame church was moved from Hodge Station to its new site in Riverside in 1892.[9] During 1906-1907, the first year that the Riverside Independent School District existed, the school for African Americans was held in Corinth Baptist Church. By 1911, the school had its own home, a two-room brick building called the Riverside Colored School, under the auspices of the Riverside Independent School District. The school became part of the Fort Worth Independent School District in 1923. The

*John Dolford "Bob" Jones was a major land owner and farmer
in the Dove community.
Courtesy Jones family and the Southlake Historical Society.*

building, no longer used as a school, still stands today at 2629 LaSalle Street.[10]

Green Loyd contributed to the development of the Riverside area in 1888 by donating a right-of-way through his land for a road connecting Fort Worth and Birdville.[11] Doubtless, the road made travel to see his daughter Malinda and other family members much easier. In its new location, Corinth Baptist Church was three miles west of the Cheneys' farm. The route from Birdville to Corinth Baptist Church went west down Belknap Street to Judkins Street; south to Ennis Avenue or south down Haltom Road (Old Goat Road); west across Beach Street (Old Negro Cemetery Road) to First Street/Fourth Street; west on Fourth to Judkins Street; then south on Judkins to the church on Ennis Avenue. Major, Malinda, and the family would be there every Sunday, and after services they would visit different families because they knew almost everyone in Riverside.

After African Americans were in this area for a number of years, there was a need for a cemetery. Trinity Chapel Cemetery (sometimes referred to as Fretwell Cemetery) is now part of a complex which also includes New Trinity Cemetery and People's Burial Park, and the three are often referred to together as New Trinity Cemetery.[12] It was in use as early as 1877, although it was not formally purchased and dedicated until 1889. This cemetery is located on NE 28th Street at the northeast corner of North Beach Street. This corner location contains the graves of several former slaves, including that of the Reverend Greene Fretwell, whose widow Frances raised thirty dollars after he died in 1886 to purchase land for a place to bury him. Using those funds, the trustees of Trinity Chapel Methodist Church bought two acres in 1889 and eventually built both a church and a cemetery. Worship services were held under a brush arbor until a frame church was built. This is where the Boaz family attended church. The Sanders, Fretwells, and Wilsons have plots in this cemetery, and the foundation of the old church building still stands today.

Dove

Dove was a rural agricultural community established during the 1870s, in an area that is now part of Southlake.[13] There were only a handful of African American families, and they typically farmed just as the white families did. One of the area's first black families was headed by a former slave named John Dolford "Bob" Jones (1850-1936). Like Major Cheney, Jones was the son of a white father (Leazer Jones) and a slave woman. As a child, Jones helped runaway slaves escape to Mexico by hiding them in a cave that is now on the edge of Lake Grapevine.[14] After the Civil War, he bought sixty acres of land from his father and established what eventually became an eleven-hundred-acre ranch. He also rode on cattle drives with civic leader E. M. "Bud" Daggett of Fort Worth, who became Jones's good friend.[15] Jones and his wife, Almeada, built a substantial two-story home on the ranch, where they raised ten children. Jones gave land for the Walnut Grove School and helped establish Mount Carmel Baptist Church. When Jones died, over five hundred people attended his funeral, including a number of whites. Mary Daggett Lake, E. M. Daggett's daughter and a Fort Worth historian, wrote a eulogy for Jones's funeral.[16] Two of his sons, John Emory Jones and Jinks Jones, continued the family's cattle business, opening a livestock auction house. The family lost a significant section of land to eminent domain between 1948 and 1952 when Lake Grapevine was built, but 266 acres today comprise Bob Jones Park, and there is an adjacent Bob Jones Nature Center.[17] Jones Park was frequently the setting for Juneteenth celebrations, which drew families from throughout Northeast Tarrant County. Other early African American families in the Dove area included farming couples William and Mille Walker and Nathaniel and Marilla Johns.[18]

Grapevine

The main African American neighborhood in Grapevine was called "Down on the Hill" or simply, "The Hill."[19] Like other small communities in Northeast Tarrant County, Grapevine was largely a farming community, so a number of the families lived on farms outside the town. Bill Jordan, a cowboy who worked for the Crabtree family for most of his life and died in 1972, was one of Grapevine's most iconic black citizens. In addition to cowboying, he also trained hunting and cattle dogs for the Crabtrees, but was most remembered for riding his huge strawberry-roan horse Baldy into Grapevine every day.[20] Sim Wright (c. 1871-1937) lived in town, although he worked on farms, and purchased a home at 417 W. Wall Street in 1917.[21] Many African Americans who didn't work in agriculture worked for the Saint Louis Southwestern Railway (Cotton Belt) or as laborers, cooks, and laundresses. Mount Horuhm Baptist Church, founded in 1905, was one of the early African American churches in Grapevine.

CHAPTER 7

The Cheney Children

In 1911, Birdville was a small, sleepy farming community with about one hundred residents. The Cheneys had many friends who lived in and around the area. Although their farm was largely self-sufficient, they relied on businesses in Birdville and Fort Worth for the few items they needed to purchase. Courtesy Tarrant County College NE, Heritage Room.

E ven though neither Malinda nor Major Cheney could read or write, they understood the importance of education. Texas moved from a frontier environment to a place where running a business—whether it was a family farm or a bank—required the ability to understand the terms of a deal and to know what you were signing. The Cheneys knew that unless their children and their neighbors' children received a good formal education, they didn't stand a chance of succeeding in a world domi-nated by educated whites. During the late 1880s, Birdville had a school for whites but did not have one for African Americans. The Cheneys met with the members of the white Birdville school board to lay the groundwork for a public school for African Americans that would follow state guidelines. The white school board appointed Ed Boaz and Oscar Loyd as trustees of the Birdville Colored School.[1] Oscar Loyd was Rush Loyd's son and Green Loyd's nephew. The school initially opened in the fall of 1888, with James W. Chapman as the teacher. He was paid $25 per month.[2]

On December 1, 1891, Major and Malinda Cheney donated one-half acre of land on which the school was built.[3] The land was located on the northwest corner of the Cheney property, where the corner of Anderson Road and Carson Street is today. The Cheneys' friend and neighbor, Ed Boaz, paid $40 to help construct the school building.[4] African American children from Riverside, Northeast Tarrant County, and Birdville attended school in this building, which opened in 1892. Several of the Cheney children attended this school, including Dollie Cheney, who completed the fourth grade there. Nun Q. Fretwell, a close friend of the Cheney family, also attended the school. Early teach-ers were Damie Brashears, W. C. Anderson, William Coleman, Maggie McEwen, and Clara Champagne, who was a close friend of Malinda Cheney.[5] Malinda would spend a month every summer at Clara's sum-mer home in Lampasas. These teachers were certified by the Birdville Independent School District and paid on a contract basis. After the school closed in 1906, some of these teachers taught at Riverside Col-ored School (now Versia L. Williams, but operating in a different loca-tion) and I. M. Terrell High School. Major Cheney remained involved with the school after it was established. He served as a trustee for the Birdville Colored School from 1902 to 1903, along with neighbors Gid Hooper and Odis Fennell.[6]

Major and Malinda Cheney's three daughters—Hattie, Mary, and Dollie—took the family's full attention as the 1880s wound down. Born a little more than a year apart in 1885, 1886, and 1887, the trio did everything together and were probably quite a handful. In the 1890s four more children, all sons, were born to Major and Malinda Cheney. They proved to be even more of a handful than the girls.

Leonidas "Lon" Cheney, born on January 26, 1890, was their first son.[7] The Cheney sons were all named after family acquaintances or well-known people. Lon was likely named for Leonidas "Lon" Barkley, son of Benjamin Franklin Barkley and his wife, Malinda. Both families may have chosen the name because Leonidas I was the king of ancient Sparta.

Landen—Lan, or John, or "Land Willie" Cheney (he had many nicknames)—was born May 4, 1893.[8] Lan was short, stocky, and good looking. He also had a serious eye for the ladies.[9] Both Lon and Lan left home at an early age, possibly because Major couldn't get much work out of them. They also had volatile tempers that got them in some serious trouble.

Polk Cheney, born on January 3, 1894, was one of Major's favorites and worked with him around the farm. Polk, named after one of Major Cheney's white half-brothers, served in the military during World War I.[10]

Major and Malinda Cheney's last child and fourth son was McKinley, born in May 1896. McKinley was somewhat spoiled and could get anything he wanted. At this time there were seven Cheney children living at home, including three older sisters who probably found baby McKinley great fun to play with. The house had plenty of room for everybody. McKinley was named after William McKinley, then the Republican candidate for president, who would become the twenty-fifth president of the United States in 1897. McKinley Cheney died of food poisoning in the year 1907, at the age of eleven. Some of Major Cheney's closest friends said that he almost went crazy as a result of his youngest child's death. Nun Fretwell, a close friend of the Cheneys, recalled that McKinley would be the first of the Cheney clan that he would take in a wagon to the community cemetery.[11]

Major Cheney understood that if his children were to be successful, it was important for him to be involved in civic affairs other than the school board. In 1899 Major Cheney was a delegate to the "colored Republican Convention" held in Austin, Texas, on October 24.[12] He also stood up for his rights in court, filing suit against Armour and Company in 1904 because he felt that runoff from the meatpacking plant was polluting the Trinity River, which was a major source of water for the family.[13] The suit was dismissed, but at that time there were few African Americans in Tarrant County who would have had the nerve to take on such a David-and-Goliath battle.[14]

On November 20, 1901, Hattie Cheney and Jimmy Sanders were married at Corinth Baptist Church by Minister W. C. Smith. Family friends Hattie and Lillie Hooper said this was one of the most beautiful weddings they had seen.[15] The couple lived in the Riverside community on Sylvania Street.

Jimmy Sanders died as the result of a terrible accident five months before his first and only child was born. James McKinley "Dick Cheney" Sanders was born to Jimmy and Hattie on September 4, 1902.[16] Jimmy Sanders had died May 27, as a result of internal bleeding. He worked for the Texas and Pacific Railway Company as a section hand. One day, while repairing the tracks, he saw that a handcar had been left on the line and noticed that a train was coming. Sanders picked up the railcar and took it off the tracks to keep other people from being injured and the railcar from being damaged. Doing so caused internal bleeding—probably an aneurysm, which killed him. This death was a crushing blow not only to Hattie, but to the whole community. Pregnant with her son, Hattie moved back to the Cheney farm to be close to her parents. Hattie would be a widow for eleven years, and her son James "Dick Cheney" Sanders would often spend time with his grandparents on the Cheney farm. James was smart and was taught well at the Riverside Colored School, which he attended between 1908 and 1914. His best subject was arithmetic, and he could calculate faster in his head than with a pencil. James also learned to speak Spanish fluently.

Hattie eventually found a new love and married Charley James, a barber, on September 20, 1913, but they were married for only seven months. On April 8, 1914, Hattie died at the age of twenty-eight. She was closely followed by her husband, who was stabbed to death on Jennings Avenue between Twelfth and Thirteenth, on March 27, 1915.[17] A man named "John Sanders," who was described as "crippled" (and James Sanders was not physically disabled), was the alleged assailant, but he was no-billed by the grand jury and never stood trial.[18] No one knows if the person responsible might have been James Sanders, but family stories mentioned that possibility because James did not care for Charley James. His mother's death left James Sanders an orphan at the age of eleven, so he moved in with his grandparents, Major and Malinda Cheney. The youngest of their own children were barely grown, but the couple willingly welcomed their eldest grandson.

Mary Cheney, Major and Malinda's second daughter, and John Guerry were married by Minister W. C. Smith on June 14, 1905, at Corinth Baptist Church. John was the son of Burton and Lottie Guerry, who lived in Riverside and were good friends of the Cheneys. John was tall and handsome, and Mary was described by Lillie and Hattie Hooper, who attended the wedding, as "cute as all get-out." The couple's oldest child, and the only one of their three to survive, was born in 1907 and named Major Guerry, after his grandfather Major Cheney.[19] John and Mary had a wonderful life, but in 1908 Mary died giving birth to a child, and the infant died as well. John Guerry was devastated, as the

Malinda Cheney flanked by her young grandsons James McKinley "Dick Cheney" Sanders, left, and Major Guerry. Thyssen family collection.

couple had been married only a little over two years. Major Guerry, the Cheney's second grandson, came to live with them at the farm.

By 1914, the Cheneys had endured the loss of seven close family members in less than two decades. Charlotte Loyd, Malinda's mother, died in 1897, and Rush Loyd, Malinda's uncle, tragically drowned in the Trinity River in 1900.[20] Major and Malinda's son-in-law Jimmy Sanders, Hattie's husband, was fatally injured in 1902. The couple then lost two of their own children, the youngest son McKinley, who died in 1907, followed by daughter Mary, in 1908. The new decade saw the death of Green Loyd, Malinda's father, who died in 1913, followed by Hattie, the couple's oldest daughter, who died in 1914. She was Major and Malinda's third child to die before her parents. Major and Malinda Cheney had been bent but not broken.

Lon Cheney married Ida May Barton at Corinth Baptist Church on May 17, 1910, when Lon was twenty-one years old. They were married by Minister A. J. Robinson. Lon and Ida lived in the Riverside area but were frequent visitors to the Cheney farm. Lan Cheney married a lady named Dessie Keith. Neither couple ever had any children.

The Cheney sons seemed to find their way into frequent scrapes with the law. The most serious incident occurred on Saturday, September 19, 1914. Lon and Polk Cheney, first identified erroneously in the newspapers as John and Poke Cheney, although "John" was later corrected to Lon, encountered a man named Lit Borders, who managed a pool hall at 284 West Thirteenth Street. According to reports, Lit Borders objected to the Cheney brothers cursing in front of his wife, and his throat was slashed. Lindsay Bell, Borders's son-in-law, chased the two Cheney brothers and fired pistol shots at them, but the shots went wild.[21] Lit Borders died later that evening.[22]

Lon was arrested the same day by a police patrolman, and Major Cheney brought Polk in the following Monday to surrender.[23] Lon said that Polk had been the one who committed the murder, so Polk was charged with murder and Lon with complicity. Polk's trial, held in October 1914, ended when one of the jurors became seriously ill, and the judge discharged the jury.[24] There is no evidence that Polk was ever retried.

Polk Cheney found himself in trouble on other occasions. On November 28, 1914, he was shot in the leg by Columbus Jackson. Polk said that the shooting was without provocation, but Jackson—and apparently a number of officers on the Fort Worth police force—believed that Polk had started the trouble. Jackson was convicted and fined $25.[25] In February 1916, Polk Cheney was arrested on aggravated assault charges stemming from an alleged attack on Ruby Daggett. Polk apparently used abusive language during the arrest and somehow had a pistol on him when he was about to be transferred from city to county jail, so those charges were added to the count.[26]

Polk Cheney joined the army when he was drafted in October 1917.[27] Although it doesn't state so explicitly, an October 28, 1917, *Fort Worth Star-Telegram* article about a group of African Americans who were drafted along with Polk Cheney implies that the draftees were a group of troublemakers who were sent away so that the military could regulate their behavior. It may have worked, because there are no further newspaper reports about Polk getting into trouble with the law. Polk married Laura Gilbert about the time that he was drafted, so he was probably pleased that the armistice was signed only a little more than a year later, on November 11, 1918. At some point in the early twenties, Polk and Laura Cheney moved to Tucson, Arizona, to live, perhaps because Polk had developed tuberculosis—the disease that would eventually kill him. The 1924 *Tucson City Directory*, which was very small, showed the couple living at 130 W. McCormick, but did not list an occupation for either person.

Polk's brother Lon Cheney had a hot temper that continued to dog him. One day while visiting at the Cheney farm, Lon instructed his nephew, James Sanders, to perform a task, using vulgar language. Lon and his wife, Ida May, were each on horseback. James and his cousin Major Guerry were the ones who were doing a good share of the work on the farm as Major Cheney grew older. James told Lon that he "wasn't his papa," and that he wasn't going to do anything. Lon became irritated and struck James with a whip. At this time everyone was calling James "Dick Cheney," a name Major Cheney had given him that recalled his own father and James's great-grandfather. James Sanders became so angry that he went to the barn and got a rifle, which he pointed at Lon. There was so much commotion and noise that the horses became riled. As James fired the gun, Ida May's horse reared up and the buckshot hit her in the wrist. James and Ida May never got along after that incident. She and Lon Cheney were eventually divorced.

In November 1915, a *Fort Worth Star-Telegram* article described Lon Cheney as a frequenter of the Battercake Flats district, a run-down residential area on the south side of the Trinity River, on the slope and at the bottom of the bluff just west of the Paddock Viaduct. Crime there was rampant. Lon was accused of aggravated assault on a police officer named J. Daniel Dennard Jr., which, according to the newspaper article, meant that Lon Cheney had cut Dennard's clothing when the officer tried to arrest him for disturbing the peace. Lon pleaded guilty and was fined $25, but was sent to the county jail because he did not have money to pay the fine.[28]

Not quite a year later, in October 1917, Lon Cheney escaped from "convict camp" and was trying to outrun a patrolman who was chasing him. The officer caught up with Cheney and attempted to arrest him, but Lon resisted—whereupon the officer took his pistol and hit Cheney on the head with his gun. The newspaper reported that "Chaney's [sic] head broke the barrel off the weapon."[29] Lon Cheney was finally captured about a month and a half later, near the edge of Battercake Flats, and returned to the convict camp on November 20, 1917.[30] Not quite

Polk Cheney wearing his World War 1 Army uniform topped by the regulation olive drab sweater. This photographic postcard image may have been taken for his family while he was at camp. Thyssen family collection.

Dollie Cheney kept the stories about life in the early Garden of Eden alive.
She outlived all of her siblings and lived on the family's land for most of her
life. Aunt Doll's face gives good clues about her character.
Sanders family collection.

four months later, following an altercation at an unnamed saloon at Belknap and Houston Streets, Will Jackson shot Lon Cheney several times through the body.[31] Cheney died on February 10, 1918, at the age of twenty-eight, from "traumatic pneumonia" (pneumonia following a penetrating wound to the lung), complicated by a gunshot wound.[32] The newspapers say nothing about whether or not the man who shot and killed him was ever brought to trial.

Major and Malinda Cheney were undoubtedly saddened not just by their son's passing, but also because of some of the choices he had made. It wasn't easy to be a hard-headed African American male in Tarrant County during the early twentieth century, when even the smallest infractions could bring harsh penalties. A hot temper could get you in even more serious trouble. Worse yet, four of Major and Malinda's seven children had now died before them, leaving an unknowable void in their lives as they grew older.

The younger of the two surviving Cheney sons, Lan Cheney, had a temper like his brothers. According to Dollie Cheney's recollections, on one occasion Lan had gotten into some trouble in downtown Fort Worth, and a fellow shot him. He wasn't killed, but his sister Dollie heard about it and went looking for the assailant. When she found the man, Dollie stabbed him and left him for dead. Nothing was ever done to Dollie for defending her brother. In some ways, Dollie was the meanest of all her siblings. She didn't back down from anyone and would fight for her brothers and sisters at any cost. Lan died of natural causes on March 24, 1921, just before his twenty-eighth birthday—the fifth Cheney child to die before his parents.[33]

James Sanders and his cousin Major Guerry were their grandparents' helpers, but James had had enough. He didn't get along with his uncles, who seemed to do only minimal work, and he didn't appreciate his mother marrying again—or dying! James had worked hard and learned a lot about farming from his grandfather, which was a useful addition to his more formal education. The only relatives he cared about were Major and Malinda Cheney and his cousin, Major Guerry. James became so distraught at some point that he decided to run away, leaving Birdville in 1914 at the age of twelve.

James rode a horse to Dallas and hopped a freight train to New Orleans, Louisiana, where he found work on a farm doing chores and odd jobs. The owner of the farm found favor in James and made him his number-one farm hand. While working in New Orleans, James was trusted to buy and sell stock, as well as purchase supplies and whatever was needed for the farm. James lived in New Orleans for two years. Everything was going well until the owner accused him of stealing. Before James could be taught a lesson, he was on the move again.

James stowed away on a riverboat. He traveled up the Mississippi River, spending time in places such as Vicksburg, Memphis, and St. Louis. In every town where he lived, James would learn a new trade. He became an avid reader, sending off for books to learn about topics that interested him—especially mechanics and machinery. James spent a lot of time in Wyoming and Montana, working on ranches and in machine shops. He became a well-traveled young man.

Around 1920, after James had been away for about six years, his grandmother, Malinda Cheney, wrote him a letter and asked him to come home. She informed him that she, Major, Polk, Dollie, and Major Guerry were about to embark on a new beginning. Fort Worth Sand and Gravel, a new company, was drawing up a contract with the Cheneys to mine sand and gravel on their property. Malinda, knowing that James was intelligent and knew something about everything, told him that he would be a perfect fit in their new endeavor. So James Sanders returned to Texas and went back to work on the farm. His grandparents were very pleased to have him back.

Among the Cheney children, Dollie Cheney was the survivor. She lived at home for many years, but was a very independent woman. The 1910 Census, when Dollie would have been twenty-three years old, shows her living with her parents and working as a cook.[34] She didn't get in as much trouble as her two brothers but, like them, she had a hot temper. A 1916 *Fort Worth Star-Telegram* listing of County Criminal Court cases notes that a "Dolly Chaney" pleaded guilty to using "abusive language" and was fined $10. A man who pleaded guilty to the same charge on the same date was fined only $1. Her tirade must have been pretty serious![35] Unlike many women of that time she waited until her early thirties to marry, wedding Raymond Dennis, who also listed his occupation as a cook, on January 9, 1920. The couple may have been together before they married, as Raymond Dennis's 1919 World War I draft registration card seems to indicate that they were a couple when he registered.[36] The couple never had any children and divorced in 1923, after being married a little over three years.[37] After Raymond Dennis's death, Dollie called herself a widow.[38]

According to family stories, Dollie traveled extensively in the American Southwest when she was young. Her travels took her to Arizona and Oklahoma while both areas were still territories, and she visited New Mexico a number of times. She probably visited her brother, Polk Cheney, and his wife Laura when she went to Arizona. Dollie told stories about working for a lady named Baird in her younger days, recounting that she did a lot of the cooking, cleaning, and baking for the Baird family. The Bairds would later form their own business and call it Mrs. Baird's Bread. According to Dollie Cheney, the recipe being used for Mrs. Baird's Bread is hers.

CHAPTER 8

Sand and Gravel

In 1903, the Chicago, Rock Island and Gulf Railway (Rock Island) built a line to the north of and roughly following the Trinity River, between Fort Worth and Dallas.[1] Part of this railway ran across Major Cheney's land, but it did not do much good in terms of helping him move his farm products to market. Railroads were the major method of moving both people and goods over long distances before paved highways and trucking systems were developed. For shorter distances, however, most people simply used wagons or carriages pulled by horses or mules. That is how Major Cheney took his produce to Fort Worth to sell. It wasn't cost effective for him to move his goods by train. Cattle and other livestock walked to Hodge Station and were sold at the stockyards.

During the early twentieth century, the roads in Tarrant County as well as in the rest of the country were largely dirt tracks following old trails. There wasn't even a proper road leading from the Cheney farm up to the Birdville Road until the end of 1911. At that point, the Tarrant County Commissioners voted to build a public road from the southwest corner of the Cheney property north to the Birdville Road.[2] Major Cheney deeded one-third of an acre of land to Tarrant County for the road right-of-way early in 1912.[3] It was not until the advent of the automobile as a preferred means of transportation that the push for good roads began. Farm wagons were one thing, but automobile drivers did not want to see their fickle vehicles shaken apart by rocky and rutted dirt roads.

Most wagon roads, like this early twentieth-century example in Northeast Tarrant County, had a dirt surface that became rough and rutted when it rained or had heavy traffic—making paved roads very attractive as automobiles and trucks replaced horse-drawn vehicles. The use of Trinity River gravel for road construction exploded during the 1920s. Courtesy Tarrant County College NE, Heritage Room.

The Federal Aid Road Act of 1916 provided for the establishment of state highway departments. The Texas Highway Department, established in 1917 and now called the Texas Department of Transportation, initially gave money to counties to build and maintain highways and roads. In 1921 an amendment to the Federal Aid Road Act provided supplemental funds for road construction and, in 1923, Texas enacted the first state gasoline tax, three-quarters of which was dedicated to road construction. As soon as the funds were in place, the movement to build roads and highways connecting Texas towns grew rapidly.[4] One of the materials that road, bridge, and building construction companies needed was gravel or aggregate to mix with a cement binder to make concrete. Gravel was also used for road and railroad beds and as a road surface.

The Cheneys prized their rich river-bottom soil because the fertile land allowed them to grow crops in abundance. In places, the soil was sandy—perfect for growing watermelons, a trademark summer crop marketed to eager Fort Worth buyers. In addition to the rich soil, however, the farmland near the Trinity River had a "substratum of rounded limestone and chert gravel" which was up to twenty-five feet thick. These deposits, located not far under the surface, were ideal for use as construction and building materials.[5]

R. M. Quigley, H. P. Bonner, and J. O. Hart recognized that land adjacent to the Trinity River had a product they needed and began to purchase or sign leases for riverbank land that had good sand and gravel deposits. Together, the three established the Fort Worth Sand and Gravel Company in 1919 and formally incorporated the firm in 1922.[6] A 1932 historical sketch of the company reads:

> When sand and gravel were first used for building roads and concrete structures in this vicinity, the pits were operated by hand and deliveries were made by wagon from pits that are now within the city limits of Fort Worth. The company is still working a number of these pits as one unit, although its operations now extend down the Trinity River about 15 miles. In 1919, the company opened the first machine-operated gravel pit in the county and produced pit-run concrete gravel for the building trade. In the following year it built a small gravity washing and screening plant in order to make a product that would compete with crushed stone.[7]

On March 26, 1921, Major and Malinda Cheney sold R. M. Quigley, who became the first president of Fort Worth Sand and Gravel Company, a fifteen-acre tract of land along the Trinity River in the W. R. Reeder Survey, for $7,500, holding the note themselves.[8] A few days later, the couple signed a ten-year contract agreeing to lease the company a strip of land forty feet wide leading across the Cheneys' land from the Trinity River to the Rock Island tracks.[9] The fifteen-acre tract was used for sand and gravel mining, and the leased strip allowed the company to build a railroad spur that hauled the mined materials to the main rail line. The lease for the strip of land paid the Cheneys $100 per year. If Fort Worth Sand and Gravel abandoned the rail spur line or let the lease expire, the company was required to remove the tracks and restore the forty-foot strip to good farming condition. Major and Malinda Cheney wanted to protect their interests, so the contract was detailed—specifying that two railroad carloads of "stock yards manure" be spread on the land as part of the restoration process and requiring a $1,000 bond to ensure compliance.[10]

The relationship was apparently beneficial for both parties. Fort Worth Sand and Gravel accessed a source of quality sand and gravel close to a rail line and to Fort Worth, while Major and Malinda Cheney, who were in their sixties, had a source of income that did not require the intensive labor of farming and livestock operations. In addition, Fort Worth Sand and Gravel provided employment for several members of the family. James Sanders, the Cheney's eldest grandson, was the first to work for Fort Worth Sand and Gravel. He began work on March 1, 1921, and retired from TXI (which acquired Fort Worth Sand and Gravel in 1953[11]) on March 1, 1971.[12] James became the chief machinist for the company, rebuilding steam engines, replacing tracks, and fixing equipment only a few steps away from his house. He worked for the company for fifty years and only missed half a day, because of the birth of his eldest son, A. J. "Buddy" Sanders, in 1923. Buddy worked for the

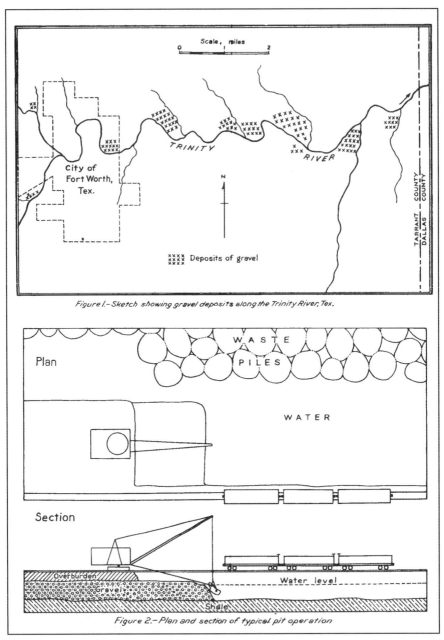

Scale, miles
0   1   2

TRINITY

RIVER

City of
Fort Worth,
Tex.

N

TARRANT COUNTY
DALLAS COUNTY

XXXX Deposits of gravel

Figure 1.- Sketch showing gravel deposits along the Trinity River, Tex.

Plan

WASTE

PILES

WATER

Section

Overburden

Gravel

Water level

Shale

Figure 2.- Plan and section of typical pit operation

A 1932 report on Fort Worth Sand and Gravel's operations illustrated the
location of gravel deposits along the Trinity River and the method that the
company used for typical pit operations. From Mining Methods And Costs At
the Hart Spur Pit of the Fort Worth Sand & Gravel Co., Inc., Fort Worth, Tex.

Fort Worth Sand and Gravel's machinery, linked by over 1,600 of feet of conveyor belts, moved, washed, and separated various sizes of gravel. The vehicle on the center right is a 1920s cement truck. Courtesy Larry Schuessler.

company for forty-seven years, between 1941 and 1988, and Buddy's son A. J. Sanders Jr., called Bubba or Drew, worked for the Fort Worth Sand and Gravel division of TXI for thirty-eight years, from 1972 until 2010.

On January 1, 1923, Major and Malinda Cheney leased a large tract of land to Fort Worth Sand and Gravel for mining operations. The biggest section of the tract included fifty acres in the southwest corner of the H. P. Tuggle Survey, where the Cheney house then stood. It also included five acres in the John Akers Survey, immediately west of and adjoining the land in the Tuggle Survey, and nine acres in the W. R. Reeder Survey, just south of and adjoining the Tuggle Survey.[13] At that time, the course of the Trinity River was different from what it is today, and the leased land was very close to the river and a prime source for

A man separates sand from Trinity River gravel using a framed hand-screening mechanism. This photograph was taken by Lenora Rolla, a longtime civic leader, historian, and founder of the Tarrant County Black Historical and Genealogical Society. Courtesy Tarrant County College NE, Heritage Room.

river gravel and sand. The lease called for payment of $500 for each acre from which sand and gravel was removed, as well as $100 per month for the ten-year length of the contract.[14] The contract also included a clause prohibiting Fort Worth Sand and Gravel from mining sand and gravel within two hundred feet of the Cheneys' house, which was located less than a mile from the Trinity River, for one year. After the first year of the contract, if Fort Worth Sand and Gravel wanted to mine near the Cheneys' residence, the company had to move the house to a different location on the farm, where it wouldn't be in the way of the excavating work.[15]

Fort Worth Sand and Gravel rapidly expanded its operations. They built the Hart Spur across the Cheneys' land to connect with the Rock Island Railway tracks and set up an operating system that would serve

Fort Worth Sand and Gravel's crushing machine, which reduced larger rocks to useable sizes. Courtesy Tarrant County College NE, Heritage Room.

them well for many years. In 1931, the company mined 341,633 tons of sand and gravel.[16] After being stripped from the banks along the Trinity, the sand and gravel were loaded into rail cars and hauled to a washing plant. Once washed, the clean sand and gravel were screened to remove pieces that were too large and then reloaded into railcars and hauled to the main line.[17] Worker salaries in 1932 ranged from thirty to seventy-five cents per hour for those involved in mining, washing, and loading operations. Wages were based on a "10-hour day and 300 working days per year." As the master mechanic, James Sanders received a monthly salary with two weeks of paid vacation per year and bonuses.[18] A salaried position placed James in the top rung of Fort Worth Sand and Gravel's organizational chart, almost unheard of at a time when teachers and ministers were nearly the only African American males who had monthly salaries instead of hourly wages. Family members also recall that he got a brand-new company truck every few years, usually blue or black, and that the company kept a small apartment for him adjacent to the Fort Worth plant so that he could shower, rest, or change clothes if he had to be away from home for an extended period.

In 1924, the Cheney house was physically moved west from its original location to the corner of Elliott Reeder Road and Carson Street, under the terms of the lease agreement with Fort Worth Sand and Gravel. This allowed the company to mine near the house's previous location. James Sanders said it took months to move the house, which was put on rollers and pulled about three miles by mules. The big house remained on that corner until it burned to the ground in 1946.

On August 4, 1925, Malinda Cheney, James Sanders, Dollie Cheney Dennis, Polk Cheney, and Major Guerry renegotiated the 1923 contract, due, in part, to the death of Major Cheney on February 14, 1925. The amount of leased land remained the same, but the terms changed. Fort Worth Sand and Gravel could mine 7.34 acres of the leased land, probably the acreage that directly fronted on the Trinity River. The lease payment was "up front," providing $6,000 in cash immediately, with the remaining $2,500 paid in installments over the next six months.[19]

When James Sanders returned to the Cheney farm in 1920 to help with farming and the sand and gravel lease, he stayed for good. He married Edith Johnson, daughter of Sarah Boaz and Jimmy Johnson and granddaughter of Ed and Aurelia Boaz, on August 26, 1922, four days after Sarah's eighteenth birthday. The two had gotten to know each other when they attended the Riverside Colored School, and the wedding ceremony was held at Corinth Baptist Church.

James and Edith lived in the Cheney house until they were able to afford their own. Major and Malinda gave their grandson and his wife a parcel of Cheney farmland as a wedding present. Later, they gave the couple a small, two-room house that they owned—probably one of the houses built for farm workers. James later added two more rooms to the structure. Like the big house, James and Edith Sanders's home was moved to its present day location, dragged over a pecan sapling which still grows in the front yard today. The house still stands at 1400 Carson Street. James and Edith Sanders had twelve children, eleven of whom survived to adulthood. All but the two youngest were born at home.

One of the owners of Fort Worth Sand and Gravel had his own plane. He would sometimes land the aircraft on James's property. James, being a machinist for the company, was adept at learning new things. He loved to tinker with machinery of any kind and was so enamored with aviation that he taught himself to fly. He would sometimes take his oldest child for a ride, flying very close to his house to wave at his wife.

CHAPTER 9

Unraveling: A New Generation
and Depressing Times

Major Cheney died on February 10, 1925, when he was sixty-nine years old.[1] He was the family patriarch and the person who oversaw the farming operations; many people depended on his knowledge and common sense. Major was also a community leader who was well known and respected by both whites and African Americans. Dr. H. B. Kingsbury, a white doctor and good friend of the family who practiced in Fort Worth but lived on Birdville Road, treated Major during his final illness. Major Cheney suffered from what was then called "acute endocarditis," a bacterial infection of the inner heart tissue, usually heart valves, which was difficult to treat. Malinda Cheney was left to manage not only the farm but also the business relationship with Fort Worth Sand and Gravel. She and Major had been married for forty-three years—more than two-thirds of her life. Only two of her seven children, Dollie and Polk, were still living, but she did have two grandchildren—James "Dick Cheney" Sanders and Major Guerry—to assist her.

Major Cheney's funeral was held at Corinth Baptist Church on February 14, 1925. Nun Fretwell, the son of Greene Fretwell, transported Major in a horse-drawn hearse to the Trinity Cemetery, where he was laid to rest in the Cheney family plot. Carl Fretwell, the son of Nun Fretwell, is the overseer of the cemetery today.

Polk, the last surviving son in the Cheney family and the one who still might have had children to carry on the Cheney name, died of tu-

Central Birdville in 1931, the year Malinda Loyd Cheney died. Courtesy Fort Worth Star-Telegram *Collection. Special Collections, the University of Texas at Arlington Library, Arlington, Texas.*

berculosis on September 17, 1926, at the age of thirty-two. At some point, he had left Arizona and returned to the Garden of Eden, so he died in Tarrant County.[2] Nun Fretwell once again transported a Cheney to Trinity Cemetery, where he was laid to rest in the family plot. Polk only had one survivor, his wife, Laura. She received Polk's benefits from his service during the First World War and lived in Arizona and then California until her death in 1978.[3]

Dollie was now Major and Malinda's only surviving child. She married for the second time, wedding C. T. Thorpe on April 10, 1926, but did not have children from either of her marriages. Loss had been a major theme in Dollie's life, and she struggled to keep afloat. Now only Malinda, James Sanders, Major Guerry, and Dollie were left to take care of the family business. The four renegotiated the Fort Worth Sand and Gravel lease and continued to farm. With income from both sources, life was a bit easier. Between the 1880s and 1926, the only

CARD OF THANKS

TO OUR many friends and neighbors:
Accept our thanks for all service ren-
dered to us during the illness and
death of our mother, Malinda Cheney.
Thanks to the following named per-
sons and societies for the beautiful
floral offerings: Mr. and Mrs. Geo.
Ringlet, Dr. Sterling White, Mrs. Della
and Mary Hooper, Mrs. Elizabeth Hol-
lingsworth, Mr. Barkley and family,
Mr. and Mrs. M. Calloway, Mrs. S. B.
Greer, Mr. and Mrs. Jesse Harper,
Mr. and Mrs. C. A. Byars, Mrs. L. F.
Caldwell, Mr. and Mrs. C. D. Rainey,
Mr. and Mrs. J. O. Hart, Mr. and Mrs.
Clifford Johnson, Mrs. Lucille Light-
foot, Miss Bessie Smith, Mr. and Mrs.
Cole, Mr. and Mrs. Smelley and son,
Mrs. J. M. Popwell and family, the
Missionary Society of Shiloh Baptist
Church, the Riverside School, Dunbar
Art Society and Charity Club. Thanks
to any whose names have been omit-
ted. The Cheney family.

The Cheney family placed this note of thanks in the Fort Worth Star-Telegram
*following Malinda Cheney's 1931 funeral. The list of names, which includes
both African Americans and whites, shows the extent of the family's friendship
network. Sanders family collection.*

mode of transportation in the Cheney family was on horseback or by
wagon. Malinda Cheney changed that in 1927, when she purchased a
brand new Studebaker automobile. It was the talk of the town, and Dollie later recounted that some folks in town even gossiped about the Cheneys and their new car. Malinda didn't have to take a written driving
test; all she had to do was prove to the police that she could drive.

Between 1925 and 1930 the Cheneys lived very well. They had
property, homes, and money. Major and Malinda didn't believe in
banks, preferring to keep their money in safe places around the house.

However, because of the lease agreement the family had signed with Fort Worth Sand and Gravel, all monies earned from lease payments were deposited directly into a bank account. This arrangement seemed to work well as long as economic times were good and the family didn't have to depend on the lease money. That story would change once the Great Depression gripped the country.

Malinda Cheney died on May 18, 1931, at the age of sixty-eight, and the family began to unravel.[4] Lillie and Hattie Hooper, childhood friends of Hattie, Mary, and Dollie Cheney, remembered the day of her death as one of the saddest days in Birdville and Riverside.[5] Malinda was very well known in the community. She had been a member in good standing at Corinth Baptist Church since its founding, and scores of people came from all around to say goodbye. It was one of the largest funerals held at Corinth, rivaling even Major Cheney's service, because Malinda was a mother to everyone. In a time when white newspapers didn't generally print obituaries for African Americans, members of the Cheney family took out a notice in the *Fort Worth Star-Telegram* to thank everyone who had assisted Malinda Cheney during her illness as well as those—including a number of whites—who had sent floral offerings to her funeral.[6] Malinda Cheney was the last member of the Cheney family that Nun Fretwell would take to New Trinity Cemetery by wagon to be buried in the family plot.

When Malinda died, Dollie Cheney, James Sanders, and Major Guerry were the only heirs. As the oldest and the last remaining Cheney, Dollie ended up with the responsibility of managing both the property and the sand and gravel operations.

Malinda Cheney's death could not have come at a worse time financially. The shock of "Black Tuesday," the stock market crash of October 29, 1929, led to ever-growing financial problems, and panic broke out when their bank went under and many of the family's financial holdings were wiped out. Malinda had been the glue that kept the Cheneys together. Dollie Cheney and her two nephews did not lose the land that Major and Malinda had accumulated for the family, but they did find that Fort Worth Sand and Gravel had not been making lease payments, and that much of the money they thought was in the bank had never been there or had been lost when the bank closed its doors.

With more limited financial resources and loans impossible to find, it became harder and harder to farm successfully and to keep up the buildings and land. The beautiful place that was known as the Cheney farm began to deteriorate. The little money that was made from the sale of sand and gravel went quickly. When Dollie discovered that Fort Worth Sand and Gravel had not been depositing the correct amount of funds into the family's bank account, she was so mad that she told the Fort Worth Sand and Gravel managers to "get your asses off my daddy's land," which meant that the company had to remove all trains, railroad tracks, boxcars, trucks, drag lines, and any other equipment used for excavation. Dollie effectively cancelled the lease and had to resort to selling sand and gravel herself.

Dollie, James Sanders, and Major Guerry began to argue with each other, eventually quarreling all of the time. Even though they still had the land, there were not enough able-bodied adult members of the family to farm all of the acreage, and there wasn't any money to pay people to work the land. No one else had ready cash, either, so when Dollie began to sell off parcels of farmland to keep everything afloat, she sold it for far less than the property had been worth only a few years earlier. It was like eating your seed corn. It helped in the short run, but created even bigger problems on down the line. Money was wasted, and relationships were ruined.

It came to a point where things had to be settled—something different had to be done. Dollie's and Major Guerry's drinking also became a problem, and that didn't help them make sound decisions. The two had become alcoholics. Perhaps it was a way to kill the pain from so much loss in the family and its rapidly deteriorating financial status. James Sanders seldom drank, and he knew that people didn't make their best decisions when they were drunk all the time. Dollie and Major Guerry were spending money like it was going out of style. Figuratively speaking, the land they owned was being given away. Any time they needed money, they would sell several acres of land, which was then no longer under the family's control.

Without Fort Worth Sand and Gravel's lease to mine sand and gravel, the sale of those resources moved to an "honor system." Independent entrepreneurs would come onto the Cheney farm and mine sand and gravel one truckload at a time. They were expected to pay for each load at the big house, and if Dollie wasn't home, the drivers were supposed to stop and leave their money in a chair on the front porch. In tight times where everyone was short of money, who knows how many truck drivers just drove on past once they saw that no one was at home? Lost revenue from several loads of sand and gravel meant that it was time to sell more land to balance the books. Dr. Kingsbury, the white doctor who had taken care of Major Cheney during his final illness, was one of the people who bought land from Dollie Cheney. He would later sell the same land back to James Sanders, but not all of the purchasers were family friends who had the family's interests at heart. James Sanders could no longer get along with his aunt and cousin, so he took it upon himself to take control of his interest in the property.

Dollie, Major Guerry, and James Sanders loved each other but could not remain in business together. In 1938, after years of squabbling, the three decided to split the remaining estate. James Sanders took one-third of the property, and two-thirds were left to Dollie Cheney and Major Guerry.[7] James also purchased a second 23.6-acre tract of land, adjacent to the land he received from the estate, from Dollie and Major Guerry.[8] Dollie Cheney's share of the land included most of the area that produced sand and gravel, while James Sanders took mainly farmland.

How could a loving family become torn apart? Greed, jealousy, and envy, marinated in alcoholism and depression, took their toll. By the end of the 1930s there was not much left of the Cheney estate. James did reclaim one piece of the former Cheney farm. After the Birdville school district closed its school for African American children in 1906, the land that had been donated by Major and Malinda Cheney stood vacant. In 1938, James Sanders requested and received title to the land.[9]

The name used by the Cheneys for their land holdings, the Garden of Eden, came into wider use during the late 1930s. Although there are scattered early twentieth-century references to white families living in the Garden of Eden, the name does not appear to have been frequently used or mapped as a geographic location.[10] In 1937, real estate developer Edward L. Baker, son of James B. Baker who ran Baker Brothers Company nursery and florists, platted land just north of the Cheney farm and called the development the Garden of Eden.[11] The lots were large, perhaps to encourage gardens or truck farms, but initially only a few were sold. More development occurred after World War II, and today a few houses remain, interspersed with warehouses and vacant lots. This area, east of Carson Street and west of Little Fossil Creek, including Garden Street and Eden Drive, was annexed by Haltom City in 1949.[12]

Major Guerry did not remain on the Cheney farm. He married a woman named Delilah "Lila" Mae Williams and moved into Fort Worth about 1940, where he worked as a laborer before joining the United States Army in May 1944.[13] The couple lived first on New York Avenue before moving to East Twelfth Street in the Riverside community, where he lived for the rest of his life. The couple never had any children. Major Guerry was self-employed for most of his career, doing everything from construction to yard work. After the war, Major Guerry

Edith Johnson Sanders and Lucinda Johnson Sadler as adults.
Sanders family collection.

Lucinda "Aunt Cindy" Sadler's water well. Garden of Eden residents re-lied on well water until 1956. Sanders family collection.

became a Christian and stopped drinking. He became a faithful member of Eastland Street Church of Christ until he died, on Independence Day, July 4, 1975.[14] He, Dollie Cheney, and James Sanders eventually reconciled, so the family that was torn apart during the Great Depression was made whole again.

Lucinda Johnson was Edith Johnson Sanders's sister. On August 21, 1926, one day after her nineteenth birthday, she married a man named Silas Robinson, but the marriage did not last. Lucinda was good looking, and Silas was a jealous man, so their divorce was only a matter of time. Aunt Cindy, as she was affectionately called, was a loving person, so she moved to the Garden of Eden to be closer to her sister. She had no children of her own, but helped Edith raise her eleven children. Lucinda worked as a professional cook at a restaurant called Georgia's Café in Birdville, and she later helped her nieces and nephews find jobs at the restaurant. Lucinda eventually married again, in 1949, wedding Hillman Sadler. She saved enough money to purchase one acre of land along Carson Street from her brother-in-law James Sanders in 1943. James, friends, and other relatives helped Lucinda build a house on that property, and she lived there until her death in 2003.

In 1946, on a Sunday morning, a tragic thing happened. The big Cheney house, lovingly built by Major Cheney, burned to the ground so quickly that hardly anything was saved. By this time, Dollie Cheney was the only person living in the big house. Bernice Sanders Jefferson, the daughter of James Sanders, was one of the first people to see the disaster as she went outside of her own home toward the outhouse. A huge fire, one she couldn't help but see, burned just down the road. Bernice ran back into her house and alerted everyone in her family including her father, her mother Edith, and all of the siblings living at home. A. J. "Buddy" Sanders, James Sanders's oldest son, and his wife Inez lived next door, and Aunt Cindy lived up the street; they were warned as well. About the same time, a neighbor named Bennie Ruth Johnson saw the fiery flames and the big beautiful house going up in smoke as she was standing in a nearby field.

Everyone ran down the road to the big house, which was fully engulfed in flames. Chaney Sanders made sure his aunt, Dollie Cheney, didn't go back into the house. She was overwhelmed and out of control. No one knew whether she was trying to retrieve her most precious mementos or wanted to die in the burning flames. It could have been either one.

It was fitting that Bernice saw the fire first. She was born in 1931, the same year that Malinda Cheney died. A calf was birthed in the cow lot on the same day. Malinda's remark was that "she didn't know who was the prettiest, that black calf in the barn or or that black girl in the house." Bernice would eventually live in a house that was given to her by Dollie Cheney. It stood on the exact spot of the old Cheney homeplace.

Processing hogs in the Garden of Eden in 1963. Sanders family collection.

CHAPTER 10

Use it up, Wear it out, Make it do . . .

W ork on the farm had by no means gotten easier. James Sanders and his family were still hunting, fishing, planting, harvesting, canning, washing, sewing, chopping wood, milking, killing hogs, and processing and smoking meat. As late as the 1940s, everything was still done by hand. The women did the housework, and the men did the work outside. Land was still cultivated with mules, horses, and plows. Everyone pitched in to harvest the crops. Farm machinery was available, but you had to have money to purchase it—and as James Sanders's children grew and had families of their own, money was in short supply.

The process of getting hogs ready for slaughter was quite interesting. The hogs were fed slop and vegetables from the garden first. After they reached four months of age, they were put on a wooden floor and fed dry corn. When the hogs were ten months old, they were the right size for slaughter. Sometimes the Sanderses would kill ten hogs at one time to provide a reliable source of meat.

It took a person who had nerves and courage to kill a hog. Once the hog was shot in the head with a .22 caliber rifle, its throat was cut immediately so that the blood could drain. Fifty gallon drums were placed into the ground at an angle (later, the drums stood on the ground and the hog carcass was lowered into the drum using an A-frame with a winch), and boiling water was poured into them. The butcher then slid the hog into the drum, completely submerging it in the boiling water. After a period of time, the carcass was removed, and the task of scraping all the hair off the hog began. The hog was then hung upside-down by its hind feet, gutted, and then butchered to separate the various cuts of meat.

Killing hogs was not the hardest job on the farm, because it was only done once a year. At least it was always done during the winter, when the weather was cooler. The hardest job on the farm was washing clothes, and the women did most of that work. The men would chop and gather wood and start the fire. They would also draw the water from the well and fill the black cast-iron wash pots, using buckets. There were two wash pots, one for washing and one for rinsing. Clothes were washed using a hard, homemade lye soap (one of the byproducts of slaughtering the hogs) and a stick to stir them in the pot. After being rinsed in clean water, they were hung out to dry. Laundry was done every Monday, depending upon the weather, because you couldn't hang clothes on the line when rain poured. With all of the work to be done, family members still had to make time to attend church and school.

Sometime during the late 1930s, a new neighbor moved into an area just east of the Garden of Eden: one of the old sand and gravel pits began to be used as a garbage dump. In 1944, Tarrant County commissioners leased the twenty-three-acre tract of land for use as a county dump, paying the owner fifty dollars per year for use of the land.[1] The Sanders family believed that sand and gravel operations provided tangible benefits, even though the mining operations and truck traffic were noisy and dirty. And James Sanders had a salaried position with Fort Worth Sand and Gravel at a time when such positions were difficult for African Americans to find. Dump operations, however, simply brought garbage down the narrow streets of the neighborhood, along with noxious odors, rutted roads, and loose litter. While garbage dumps were frequently located in rural areas, it was not uncommon to place them near "people who didn't complain"—often people of color who didn't have the time or connections to protest.

*James "Dick Cheney" Sanders in front of the Sadler House on his beloved
International Harvester Farmall tractor. Sanders family collection.*

By the late 1940s James Sanders was finally able to invest in equipment to make farm work easier. He bought an International Harvester
Farmall tractor that cranked from the outside, with the plows, planters,
disk, mechanical scythe, hay baler, and rake that went with it. The Farmall was an affordable, all-purpose tractor that allowed farmers on small
and medium family farms to mechanize their operations. Sanders was
a machinist by trade, so if anything broke, he fixed it. He could also
make the parts if they wore out. When the corn was harvested, Sanders
attached his grinding machine to the tractor's belt pulley and ground
the kernels into cornmeal. He pumped water from the Trinity River and
irrigated his crops when needed. Sanders farmed less land than his
grandfather, and he was also able to take advantage of the time- and

labor-saving devices that Major Cheney never dreamed of, so that he could both farm and work full-time for Fort Worth Sand and Gravel. Sanders and his sons cut their own posts to build fences and, when formerly domesticated hogs escaped other farms and became feral—destroying Sanders's fields—he enclosed his crops with an electric fence.

With so many mouths to feed—James Sanders and his wife Edith had twelve children, eleven of whom survived to adulthood—getting enough food on the table was always a challenge. Chickens matured quickly, so Sanders decided to raise them intelligently. He built a chicken house and installed an electric brooder. Chicks would stay in the chicken house until they were about two months old, when they moved to the yard. They provided meat, eggs, and more chickens.

Sanders loved machinery and made many of the tools that he used on the farm. Among them were a table saw, a gas-powered tree-cutting saw on wheels, metal feeding troughs, and his own metal toolbox. He made A-frames that were strong enough to winch cars, hogs, and other heavy items. Nothing went to waste. Malinda's old car frame was turned into a trailer base, and Sanders made his own camper for his pickup. Not everything was used for work. He also built a miniature train powered by a steam engine. His oldest son, A. J. "Buddy" Sanders, and the grandchildren witnessed the test run. Sanders was the first person in the Garden of Eden to buy a radio, a television, and a washing machine. Not only did he make life easier for his wife Edith, but also for a lot of folks in the neighborhood. When something went wrong with one of these modern gadgets, he could fix it.

Faith and spirituality were always an important part of life in the Garden of Eden. The family had long attended Corinth Baptist Church, but in 1949, a new church was established on what is now Elliott Reeder Road. Dollie Cheney sold some of her land to Birdville Baptist Church, which started Valley Baptist Church as a mission. Its wood-frame building was completed in 1951 and first held services that March.[2] That structure was replaced by a brick building in 1963.[3]

Above: *Hillman Sadler, Lucinda Johnson Sadler's husband, with his chickens.*
Below: *The first Valley Baptist Church structure was a utilitarian wood-frame building erected in 1951 on Elliott Reeder Road. Garden of Eden residents provided much of the labor to construct the church, and family members moved their membership from Corinth Baptist to Valley Baptist, which was within walking distance of their homes.*
Both photographs, Sanders family collection.

Above: *Florence, Jolene, Zimmie, and James Ross with baskets of greens on the Bussey farm, which was just east of the Garden of Eden.*
Left: *Jodie and Florence Ross picking greens on the Bussey farm. Both photographs circa 1940s. Sanders family collection.*

Family members could now walk to church, and after services, gather for one of the family's celebrated Sunday dinners. Reverend E. E. Warren served as the first pastor of Valley Baptist Church, and Reverend Brown, Reece Williams, Reverend Warren, Herbert Johnson, A. J. Sanders, Delbert Sanders, Edward Sanders, and Isiah Wilson helped build the church. James "Dooney" Sanders was not old enough to help with the construction work, but he served as a "poster child" for the benefits that the church could bring the community. Both his photograph and in-person visits were used to show that this "young, smart black child and his future (religious and otherwise) are what Birdville [Baptist Church] would be investing in if they sponsored the black church."[4]

Great-great-grandchildren were baptized and raised in the church. Even if their parents had moved to Fort Worth or another nearby town, the family came back to worship at Valley Baptist. As the amount of land comprising the Garden of Eden grew smaller, and industrial uses encroached on the tranquility of the area, the church helped keep the family's sense of place strong.

There was never a dull moment in the Garden of Eden. The farm was still fairly isolated, and Sanders was very protective of his crops. He didn't want anything disturbing this valuable piece of property, whether man or beast. On March 13, 1953, the *Fort Worth Star-Telegram* ran a page-one article headlined, "$10,000 Horse is Found Dead, Mutilated with Two Others." A man who owned two of the horses said that they had been placed to graze in a leased pasture in the Trinity River bottoms south of Birdville, and after the animals did not appear for feeding for two days, he discovered their bodies covered with brush and partially burned.[5]

By the following morning, more of the facts had come to light. James Sanders told two sheriff's deputies that he had killed the three horses, which he thought were "soapers," or animals in poor condition not fit for any type of work, after they had been turned loose in his fields. Sanders said that he had shot the horses only after they entered his garden plot and eaten his corn.[6]

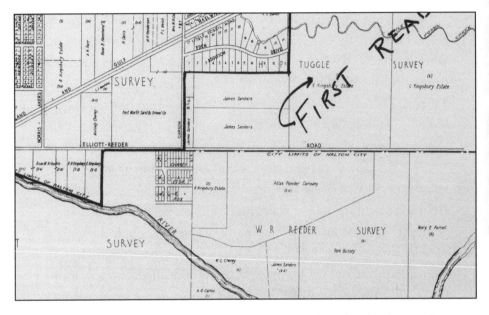

This detail from a 1959 Rady map of Haltom City shows how land ownership in the Garden of Eden changed in the decades after Major and Malinda Cheney died. Courtesy Special Collections, the University of Texas at Arlington Library, Arlington, Texas.

Sanders told family members the rest of the story. A man had asked if he could graze his horses in Sanders's fields, but Sanders explicitly told the man that he did not want any livestock grazing on his property. Several days later, Sanders happened to walk down to the bottom after work and discovered that his fences had been cut in such a way that it appeared that livestock had broken through the fence. Sanders also discovered horses grazing on his property. He then told his son, Delbert Sanders Sr., to go to the owner's home and tell him to remove the horses. In the meantime, Sanders started to gather the horses. When they broke and ran, smashing his garden, he grabbed his Winchester and shot each one of the horses in the head.

Sanders then instructed Delbert, Edward, and their cousin "Bit"

James and Edith Sanders's children and their spouses gathered for this family portrait, taken in 1962. Back row, left to right: Henry Gentry, Dollie Sanders Gentry, A. J. "Buddy" Sanders, Inez Sanders, Delbert Sanders Sr., Beverly Sanders, Bob Ray Sanders, Hattie Mae Sanders Sedberry. Front row, left to right: James M. Sanders Jr., Chaney Sanders Sr., Joan Sanders, Floyd Jefferson, Bernice Sanders Jefferson, Chamberlin "Chink" Sanders, Josephine High Sanders, Dan Moody Russell, Virgil Lucinda Sanders Russell, and Edward Sanders. Sanders family collection.

Wilson to get the tractor and drag the horses to the riverbed. The boys did what Sanders told them to do. When the dead horses were found, the sheriff's deputies came for James Sanders. He wasn't in hiding, and they didn't have to hunt far or long, because he was at work at Fort Worth Sand and Gravel. When asked if he had shot the horses Sanders, without any hesitation, admitted to the shooting and said that if the owner had been there he would have shot him too. He further explained that he expressly denied permission for the horses to be on his property and that they were there illegally. The authorities at Fort Worth Sand and Gravel supported James Sanders 100 percent, and no charges were ever filed.

By the late 1960s, indoor toilets were finally installed in the Garden of Eden houses where the members of the Sanders family lived. They still didn't have city sewer lines, so they had to install their own septic systems. But what a wonderful convenience!

More Dollie Cheney Stories

I didn't really become acquainted with my great-great aunt until I was about five years old. The memories of Aunt Doll will always be with me. She taught me how to read before I started to school. She would have me to go out in the yard and get the newspaper and then sit me on her lap so that she could read to me. It didn't take long for me to catch on. What an amazing lady! Aunt Doll was sixty years old when I was born in 1947.

When I was in the sixth grade, I remember asking her questions about her family. When Aunt Doll was in a good mood, she would talk for hours. She really knew her family history, and many of the family stories in this book came directly from her lips. From the time I was eleven years old until the time she died, I was constantly asking her questions.

Some other events that I will never forget about Aunt Doll were the way she would pull Bob Ray's and my teeth. When our baby teeth became loose, she would get a piece of thread, loop it around the loose tooth, and yank it out. She was our first and only dentist for a while. Aunt Doll would also treat our insect bites with the most inexpensive ointment, snuff! She always dipped snuff, so whenever some was needed, she would put her fin-

In spite of Dollie Cheney's outsize character and impact on the lives of her family members who lived in the Garden of Eden, there are relatively few photographs of her. Despite its fuzziness, this photo shows Aunt Doll as I remember her later in life. Sanders family collection.

ger in the bottom of her lip and scoop out a finger full and apply it to the insect bite. Not only would it cure the sting, but it would soothe it also.

Aunt Doll had very long hair. When it was combed straight back it would flow past the center of her back. She would let the children comb her hair. This was probably soothing and relaxing.

Bob Ray and I would also spend the night with Aunt Doll; Bob Ray more than I. This was a task that both of us hated. There were reasons we hated this, one was that she went to bed around 6:00 p.m. and awoke the next day before 5:00 a.m. The other reason we hated to sleep with her was because she would always wet the bed. This was not a pleasant feeling. We would have to get up the next day, change the sheets, take the wet sheets outside, and hang them on the clothesline. Sometimes this unwanted displeasure would happen late at night and you would have to lie there until the next morning.

Another chore that Bob Ray and I had to do for Aunt Doll was to run and get the mail. During this time the mailbox was located on the corner of Haltom Road and Elliott Reeder Road. We had to run west on Elliott Reeder Road for a mile and then back (two miles round trip), six days a week. I guess that was one of the reasons we became good runners. In spite of all of these things we had to do for Aunt Doll, we still had chores to do at home.

James and Edith Sanders, my grandparents, made it possible for Aunt Doll to have a place to live. The Cheneys owned houses that their hired hands had lived in back in the 1920s. With the help of family members and friends, James Sanders moved one of those small houses to the spot where the old homeplace had stood. Aunt Doll lived in this house until the 1970s.

Aunt Doll's mind remained sharp until the day she died. Even in her 80s when I would go by and visit her, she would ask me to bring her a half pint of whiskey to get her through the day. I had to go all the way to the package store at Six Points in Riverside to get what she wanted. She would always tell me that a little whiskey wouldn't hurt you. Some of her favorite meals included lamb chops for dinner; pork chops, eggs, and toast *for breakfast; and cornbread and buttermilk mixed together in a tall jar or glass for a late-night snack.*

Aunt Doll became ill in her old age. James and Edith took care of her for a couple of years, but she became so sick that they couldn't care for her anymore. She was moved to a nursing home where she remained until her death at the age of eighty-seven. Aunt Doll lived longer than any of her family members. Dollie Cheney died on January 22, 1974.[7] Her funeral was held at Valley Baptist Church, which was located in the Garden of Eden on property that she sold to the church. The service only lasted an hour. She was buried at the Community Cemetery in the family plot and was the last of the Cheneys.

Choice Aunt Doll sayings:

"Hell, I went by the schoolhouse even if I didn't stop."
"Now don't get so drunk that you can't smell my whiskey."
"She couldn't buy a mosquito a head rag."
"I'd rather see it than hear about it."
"Just a little bit of his gravy runs all over my plate."
"He makes my ass want to take a dip of snuff."
"If I tell you a hen dips snuff, check under its wing and see if you don't find a can of Garrett."

Joe Louis Addition

In January 1948, a man named Ben R. King sold a parcel of land in the northeast corner of the Samuel Elliott Survey to a man named Eulice Foy "Slick" Abbott.[8] The land, located just south of Carson Street and Elliott Reeder Road and north of the Trinity River, had once belonged to Dollie's great-uncle, Rush Loyd. His daughter-in-law, Sadie

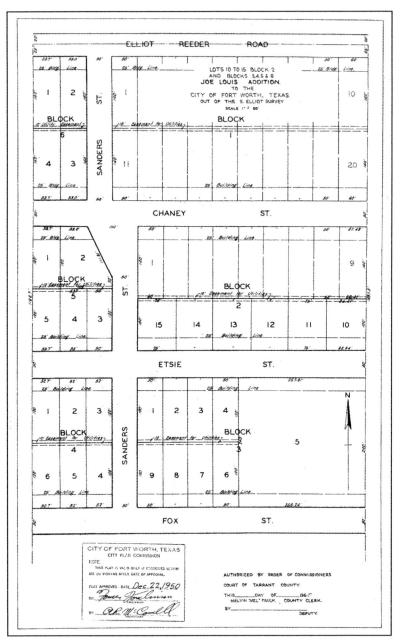

The 1950 plat map for the Joe Louis Addition, filed on January 21, 1951, shows lines for the placement of utilities, but water lines were not put in when the homes were constructed. Fox Street, the southernmost street on the map, was never used. Courtesy Tarrant County Clerk's office.

Haltom City put in the only sources of drinking water for Joe Louis Addition residents—a handful of outdoor faucets with hoses attached.
Courtesy Texas Observer.

Loyd, sold the land to family friend Robert Kingsbury, a gravel operator, in 1915, after her own husband's death, and over the years it had been used as a cornfield, passing through a number of owners.

After World War II, housing was in short supply as soldiers came home and wanted a place to settle down and start their families. This was particularly true for African Americans, who had fewer options because they could not rent or buy in areas where whites lived. E. F. Abbott told Dollie Cheney that he wanted to build something "nice for the colored people who needed housing." He knew the Cheney-Sanders family because he owned the Abbott and Newman Sand and Gravel Company, as well as the Fort Worth Concrete Company, and had bought sand and gravel from the family after the contract with Fort Worth Sand and Gravel expired. Nevertheless, the land was not under direct family control, so they could only make suggestions about what was planned.

Edith Boaz Sanders was instrumental in naming the community after Joe Louis, the famous boxer, who was the heavyweight champion at the time. During this time, Joe Louis was a hero to all people of color. The Joe Louis Addition opened in the spring of 1948. Abbott's original advertisements, which ran in the *Fort Worth Star-Telegram* between mid-1948 and early 1951, first offered lots for sale and then homes that were either for sale or for lease.[9] The ads either appeared in a separate "colored" real estate section, or the property was identified as being for "coloreds." Although families immediately bought and occupied the houses, E. F. Abbott did not file a plat for the land until January 21, 1951.[10] He indicated on the plat that the development was located in Fort Worth, but in fact it was in unincorporated Tarrant County at the time and had no municipal utility services.

Most of the houses were constructed the same way, basically two or three-room wood-frame houses, with no running water or bathrooms. There were only four streets in this neighborhood, and Slick Abbott had a hand in naming them. Sanders Street ran north and south, while Chaney Street (definitely *not* spelled the way the family spelled their name), Etsie Street, and Fox Street ran east and west. Fox Street was never built on. Elliott Reeder Road was the northern boundary. Even though the land wasn't in Haltom City, that municipality eventually put in a handful of outdoor water faucets to provide drinking water. Imogene Smith, one of the early residents, remarked, "We had a lovely community, really. But some of 'em lost their houses through fallin' behind in their payments. Others were able to move on to better places and some, you know, had to move for the conveniences. You can't get the bus here." The tiny neighborhood grew from only four houses in the late 1940s to an estimated 200 people at its height in the late 1950s. [11]

In 1954, John William "Bill" Estes, who had been involved with

Mrs. C. B. Carey, who lived at 5404 Etsie in the Joe Louis Addition, paid $35 a month for seventeen years toward the purchase of her home. Her house was tagged as "substandard" and demolished in 1970 while she was away caring for a daughter's children. Courtesy Texas Observer.

his family's waste hauling business in Arizona, moved to the Haltom City area and established the Estes Service Company.[12] The company quickly took over waste disposal services for a number of small communities in Tarrant County, and using the landfill next to the Garden of Eden and the Joe Louis Addition, built itself into one of the largest waste haulers in the county. Through a man named J. C. Estes, Bill Estes bought the dump property in 1958.[13] Tarrant County also used the dump for county garbage and, in 1967, installed an incinerator at the Estes Dump in an effort to extend landfill capacity.[14] In 1969, an investigation undertaken by Tarrant County to study the use of county employees and equipment at the private landfill recorded "an average of

*Tarrant County and the Estes Dump partnered to build an incinerator to re-
duce the smell of decomposing garbage and save landfill space. The
incinerator, shown here being assembled in 1967, spewed a fine black ash over
the Garden of Eden and the Joe Louis Addition soon after it began operating.
Nearby residents complained, but their protests had little impact. It was not
until complaints from white neighborhoods and allegations of inappropriate
use of county employees and machinery at the dump that the
incinerator was finally taken out of service.*
Courtesy Fort Worth Star-Telegram *Collection. Special Collections,
the University of Texas at Arlington Library, Arlington, Texas.*

10 Estes Service Co. trucks an hour . . . 10 hours a day" hauling waste
to the landfill.[15] The dump was not a pleasant neighbor to have, especially when your own home had no trash collection service.

After residents spent several years making their monthly mortgage
payments, Slick Abbott sent out eviction notices to almost everyone in
the neighborhood. He invoked a clause in the sales contract which said

if the buyer was ever late with a payment (the "grace" period was only five days), then the sale of the property was cancelled and all other payments would be considered only as rent or lease payments.[16] People thought they had been buying their homes, but most (because they had been late on a payment) were only leasing and eventually lost their homes.

People didn't understand why Slick Abbott was so eager to get the property back. There had been talk for many years about channelizing the Trinity River for navigation, and the area where the Joe Louis Addition was located was on planning maps as a preferred site for a turning basin—something that would make the land valuable if the plans came to pass.[17] But in fact, the Estes Service Company dump needed more land to expand, and Abbott was hoping to sell the Joe Louis Addition land to them. Fort Worth and Haltom City also wrangled over control of the Trinity River bottomland, and following a court fight, Fort Worth annexed the neighborhood in 1969.[18] At that point, the residents started paying property taxes to the City of Fort Worth, but didn't receive city water because it would have "cost too much" to run pipes to the small neighborhood. Trash collection consisted of a single large dumpster that was emptied only when residents complained. Why no regular trash pickup? Well, you had to have water service so that the fee for trash collection could be added to your water bill.[19]

In October 1967, the incinerator at the nearby Estes Dump malfunctioned, clouding the neighborhood with acrid smoke.[20] As the already-substandard homes declined, Fort Worth began an aggressive program to demolish the structures, but the rubble was typically abandoned on site.[21] The well-known journalist Molly Ivins wrote an exposé of the deplorable living conditions in the Joe Louis Addition for the *Texas Observer* in 1970. By then, Slick Abbott had washed his hands of the whole development. A man named R. R. Billings ended up holding many of the leases, and the City of Fort Worth pressed him to bring substandard residences up to code. Mrs. C. B. Carey, who lived at 5404 Etsie but who was staying with a married daughter to help out with child care, had been paying $35 a month for her home since September 15, 1953. Billings received a notice about her property on March 18, 1970, and after a series of missteps and miscommunications, the house was bulldozed, with Mrs. Carey's possessions buried under the rubble. The city's inspection reports had mistakenly said that no furniture or belongings were in the house and that it was vacant.[22] By the mid-1980s most of the folks had moved out of the neighborhood, leaving it to auto wrecking yards and the nearby garbage dump. Only a handful of families still live in the Joe Louis Addition.

These were the names of the families that lived in the Joe Louis Addition:

> Mr. & Mrs. Cato Adams and family
> Mrs. Mary Allen and family
> Mr. & Mrs. Baldwin
> Mr. & Mrs. A. J. "Biggum" Blaylock and family
> Mr. & Mrs. Jack Blaylock and family
> Mr. & Mrs. Jeff Brown and family
> Mr. & Mrs. Joe Brown and family
> Mrs. Nadine Brown and family
> Ms. Calton and family
> Mr. & Mrs. Preston Carey and family
> Mr. & Mrs. Caruthers and family
> Mr. & Mrs. Henry Covington and family
> Mr. & Mrs. Ruben Crane and family
> Mr. & Mrs. Ollie Duckett and family
> Mr. & Mrs. Samuel Duckett and family
> Mr. & Mrs. Elder and family
> Mr. & Mrs. Marshall Evans

Mr. Herman Ford and family

Mr. & Mrs. Nash Ford and family

Mr. & Mrs. Oscar Ford and family

Mr. Gomillion French and family

Mr. & Mrs. Willie Gilstrap and family

Otis & Martha Hall

Bo High

Shirley High

Rev. Jackson and family

Mr. & Mrs. Floyd Jefferson and family

Mr. & Mrs. Homer Jones and family

Mr. & Mrs. Y. D. Jones and family

Mr. & Mrs. Ray McCarver and family

Mr. & Mrs. Eddie McDonald, Willie Esther and family

Mrs. Catherine Miller and family

Ms. Billie Phillips and family

Ms. Ellen Phillips and family

Rev. Isaiah & Margaret Rice

Ruben & Dora Russell and family

Mr. & Mrs. Chaney Sanders and family

Mr. & Mrs. Robert "Pa" Shaw and family

Harry & Imogene Smith and family

Mr. & Mrs. James Sneed

Mr. & Mrs. William Sneed and family

Mr. & Mrs. Ollie Snell and family

Mr. & Mrs. Will Veasley and family

Mr. & Mrs. Pete Walton and family

Lula V. Watts

Mr. & Mrs. Roscoe Weatherd and family

Mr. & Mrs. Lee Wilson and family

Mr. & Mrs. Clift Wright and family

CHAPTER 11

A New Generation of Sanderses

*The North Side Colored School shown here in 1921, just before it was
renamed in honor of longtime teacher and principal Isaiah Milligan Terrell,
served as a combination middle and high school until 1938, when a former
white school was rebuilt and expanded as I. M. Terrell High School.
Courtesy Tarrant County College NE, Heritage Room.*

T he Cheneys had not been
taught to hate but were
taught to love and forgive.
When Major and Malinda's children were not allowed to attend the
white schools in Birdville because of segregation, the couple helped
found the Birdville Colored School. Between 1891 and 1906, children
who lived in the Garden of Eden or in surrounding communities, including the Cheneys, Boazes, Loyds, and Fretwells, attended the
Birdville Colored School, which was located on land donated by Major

Cheney. When the colored school closed in 1906, children then attended the Riverside Colored School from the first through the eighth grade, and high school at the North Side Colored School No. 11 on East Twelfth and Steadman streets in Fort Worth.[1] Isaiah Milligan Terrell served as principal of this school from 1906 to 1915. The school was named I. M. Terrell High School in 1921, in honor of its former principal. The school at Twelfth and Steadman became an elementary and junior high school called George Washington Carver Elementary / Junior High School in 1938, when an expanded I. M. Terrell High School building opened at 1411 E. Eighteenth Street. High school students from the Garden of Eden attended Terrell until 1965, when Haltom City schools integrated. Fort Worth schools finally integrated in 1973, and I. M. Terrell High School was closed. It reopened as an elementary school in 1998 and still serves that purpose today.[2]

As the crow flies, the Garden of Eden was a little over four miles from the Riverside Colored School and about five and one-half miles

Historically, there were two Riverside Elementary schools—one reserved for white students and the other for African American students. Children in the Sanders family attended this school because they could not take classes at the closer white elementary school in Haltom City. Students are dressed for a May Day celebration in this 1950s photograph. The school is now named for Versia L. Williams, who worked at the school as a teacher and principal for forty-six years. Sanders family collection.

from the North Side Colored School and I. M. Terrell High School. There were no buses to transport black students to school—you either walked or were transported by car. James Sanders drove a company truck, and Edith drove a Buick, so Edith had the privilege of driving the neighborhood children to school. She started out driving to the Riverside Colored School. As the children grew older, Edith Sanders added the North Side Colored School (later Carver Elementary/Junior High), and then I. M. Terrrell High School, to her route. At times there were as many as fourteen children riding in the car, sitting on each other's laps without seat belts![3] That meant two round trips a day, long before the Airport Freeway offered a relatively straight shot into town. It seemed like such a waste of time and money, sometimes stopping at three places to drop off or pick up children, when there were schools in the neighborhood less than two miles away. The sacrifice was made, and the children rarely missed a day of school.

Nine of James and Edith Sanders's eleven surviving children graduated from high school. Chaney and Edward Sanders each left school early to enter military service. Chaney joined the army and fought in the Korean War. Edward joined the navy and was honorably discharged in California, where he lived until his death. As Dollie Cheney sold off land, and the size of the farm shrank, it could not support all of James and Edith Sanders's children and their families. Farming also became more mechanized, and that meant that less sweat equity was needed to plant, cultivate, and harvest crops. Urban life also became an attractive option for children in farm families. They saw more opportunities to use their education in a town or city setting, whether they worked in manufacturing, the service industry, or held a professional position. Military service also taught many practical skills that could be used to earn a living outside of farm work in civilian life.

After leaving the army, Chaney Sanders, James and Edith Sanders's fourth child, returned home and married Lilly Roberson, and the cou-

I. M. Terrell High School, shown in 1939 shortly after it opened, served as the only high school in the region for African American students until integration closed the school in 1973. For decades, Edith Sanders drove her own children and others from the neighborhood into Fort Worth so that they could get a high school education. Courtesy Fort Worth Star-Telegram Collection. *Special Collections, the University of Texas at Arlington Library, Arlington, Texas.*

ple had two children before divorcing. Later, Chaney married Joan Holbert, and together they had five children. Chaney was employed by Gulf Oil Company and worked there for forty years. Like his father, Chaney was a jack-of-all-trades who could fix anything. He was also a great swimmer and fisherman who taught a growing number of children the secrets of fishing.

Edward Sanders, the couple's seventh child, settled in Los Angeles after completing his navy service and married his childhood sweetheart, Rosa Lee Bettis, from Fort Worth. Edward was a musician who played piano and guitar. He worked as a machinist and sheet metal worker for the Veteran's Administration. Edward loved the game of pool, played well, and had his own personalized cue. Rosa attended Compton College in Compton, California (part of the metro Los Angeles area), and received both her licensed vocational nurse and registered nurse licenses. She later attended Charles R. Drew University of Medicine and Science, where she was one of the first African American females to become licensed as a physician's assistant.

Below: A. J. "Buddy" Sanders played both offense and defense on the 1940 I. M. Terrell High School Panther varsity football team. The team won the Prairie View Interscholastic League state championship, the high school football title for African American schools. Sanders family collection.

TERRELL HIGH RATING			
Terrell—	—Opponent	Terrell—	—Opponent
Terrell 41	Ennis 0	Terrell 21	Lincoln (Dallas) 0
Terrell 12	Jackson (Corsicana) 0	Terrell 0	Douglas (Okla. C.) 0
Terrell 6	Washington (Dallas) 7	Terrell 0	Washington (Houston) 2
Terrell 37	Washington (CWF 0	Terrell 19	Ardmore 0
		Terrell 19	Yates (Houston) 7

Terrell 15 .... Lincoln (Dallas) 6
Terrell 33 .... Scott (Tyler) 0
Terrell 26 .... Austin 0

STANDING TOTAL

Terrell 201 .... Opponents 22

A. J. "Buddy" Sanders celebrating his high school graduation in 1941. Sanders family collection.

In 1941, A. J. "Buddy" Sanders and Hattie Mae Sanders became the first of James and Edith Sanders's children to graduate from I. M. Terrell High School. There were certain advantages to going to a "big city" high school, even if it meant hurrying through your farm chores and staying up late to make sure all your homework was done correctly. Buddy, the oldest of the couple's children, was the first of the Sanders boys to play varsity football for the Terrell Panthers. He played both offense and defense on the 1940 I. M. Terrell High School State Football Championship team, in the first Prairie View Interscholastic League (PVIL) championship playoffs.

After graduation, Buddy dreamed of attending Tuskegee Institute so that he could become a pilot and fight for his country during World War II. The institution was famous for training 994 black airmen, 450 of whom served overseas during the war. After his father explained that the family could not afford college, Buddy was heartbroken, but understood. He would say to himself, "If you want to become successful in life, you'd better stop feeling sorry for yourself and get you a job." Buddy began to work at Fort Worth Sand and Gravel in 1941 and didn't retire until 1988. He also worked a second job in the Swift meatpacking plants on the North Side. With income from two jobs and no family to support, Buddy was able to save up enough money to buy some cattle and a 1937 Ford convertible.

When he wasn't working, Buddy was boxing. He was pretty good, and his father would take him to different communities and match him against the best fighter each place had to offer. Ninety-five percent of the time, Buddy would win. People said that he was a sharp dresser and had plenty of money. He frequently hung out with older people.

Buddy and his '37 Ford were always together. He loved to explore, driving the roads of North Texas to see what he could find. Eventually, he stumbled upon a little town in Dallas County called Bear Creek, which was another freedmen's community, located about twenty-five miles east of Birdville. There, Buddy met a woman named Inez Trigg and fell head over heels in love with her. He began to go to Bear Creek every weekend, flying down the road as fast as his convertible would take him. A trip to Bear Creek from Birdville would only take Buddy about twenty minutes.

One Saturday night, after courting Inez, Buddy drove home so fast that it seemed like he was outrunning the wind. He always drove with

The Bear Creek community, located in western Dallas County and now a part of Irving, was home to sisters Inez and Opal Trigg. They attended the Bear Creek School shown here. Inez married A. J. "Buddy" Sanders, and brought "Aunt Opal" Trigg Woods with her to be part of the family.
Courtesy Tarrant County College NE, Heritage Room

his left arm hanging outside of the car. Traveling down Highway 183 between Bear Creek and Mosier Valley, without modern highway lights, Buddy hit two mules standing in the road and killed both of them instantly. Buddy almost met his maker, too.

By the time the police and ambulance arrived, Buddy Sanders was barely hanging on. His left arm was severely mangled, and he was in shock. The ambulance rushed Buddy to the City-County Hospital in Fort Worth, where the attending physician told him that they would have to amputate his arm. James and Edith Sanders didn't find out about the accident until early the next morning, but when they did, they rushed to the hospital. Buddy was awake and worried about losing his arm. He pleaded with his mother and father to find a doctor who could

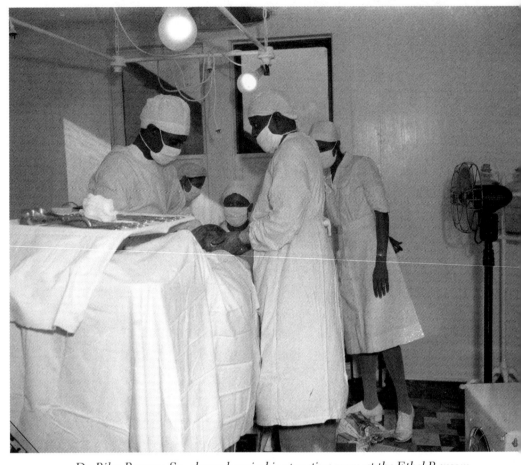

Dr. Riley Ransom Sr., shown here in his operating room at the Ethel Ransom Memorial Hospital, was the surgeon who performed delicate reconstructive surgery on A. J. "Buddy" Sanders's arm. Courtesy Marion Butts Collection, Texas/Dallas History & Archives Division, Dallas Public Library.

save it. Time was of the essence, because Buddy had lost a lot of blood, and the doctors didn't want an infection to set in.

Inez Trigg's older sister, Opal, heard about the accident and told Inez, saying, "You know that little red guy you been seeing; well, he was almost killed in a car accident last night."[4] Then Inez went into shock!

The family reached out to Dr. Riley Ransom, a well-known Fort Worth African American physician and surgeon. He told everyone that he could operate to save Buddy's arm, but that it would never be fully functional. It took hours for Dr. Ransom to piece the tendons, nerves, muscles, and what was left of the bones back together. He manipulated the bone fragments back into place and secured them with wire. Buddy was in the hospital for more than a month, and off work for almost a year, but he regained full use of his left arm and went back to work for Fort Worth Sand and Gravel, driving a new car. A large scar on his left arm remained to remind Buddy how close he was to death that night.

Buddy Sanders married Inez Trigg on June 16, 1944. James and Edith Sanders gave the couple a half-acre tract of land next to their own home as a wedding present. Buddy bought some milk cows and put them out on his father's farmland to graze so that everyone could have fresh milk and butter. Buddy and Inez lived with his great-aunt, Dollie Cheney, when they first got married, but Buddy, James, and other family members helped build the couple their own house on the half-acre lot.

Inez, who came to be called Mama 'Nez, was a welcome addition to the family. She became pregnant with their first child at the same time that James and Edith Sanders were expecting their last baby. Inez gave birth to Andrew J. "Drew" Sanders, the author of this book, nine days before Edith delivered Bob Ray Sanders, making the nephew older than his uncle. Edith and Inez raised the two boys together, spending hours lovingly tending their babies and often dressing them alike—as though they were twins—with sometimes hilarious results. Bob Ray Sanders wrote a column about one such incident:

> I shall never forget one day as we rode on the back of the bus headed to the old Ritz Theater [sic] downtown and dressed in our identical matching shirts and shorts, a woman asked, "Who's the oldest?"

We responded at the same time.

"He is," I said while Andrew responded (pointing to himself), "I am. I'm nine days older than he is."

I could see the anguish on the lady's face as she wondered how a mother had endured such a painful delivery over such a long period of time.[5]

Buddy and Inez had eight children together, and Mama 'Nez grew from caring for her family to caring for the community as a whole. She continued the tradition of Sunday dinners, coordinated church fundraising, served as president of the I. M. Terrell Parent Teacher Association (PTA), was a member of the Eastern Star, watched over the growing brood of Cheney great-grandchildren, and formed the Sanders-Trigg Family Choir—a gospel choir—which was active for thirty years. Buddy and Inez were married for fifty-five years and lived in their Garden of Eden home for the rest of their lives.

Hattie Mae Sanders, Buddy and Inez's second child who was named for her great aunt, earned academic honors in the classroom. She was only four years old when she started school, so she graduated from Terrell two years early. After graduation, Hattie Mae worked at the Ritz Theatre at 909 Calhoun in downtown Fort Worth. Today, the site of this segregated theater, which served Fort Worth's African American citizens, is a parking lot. Hattie Mae saved her money and moved to Los Angeles in 1946, where she married her hometown boyfriend, Alwyn Sadler, who was a cook. They later divorced. Hattie Mae also worked as an executive chef for Litton Industries and as a caterer, and she fell in love with the people and the climate of California. After moving to Los Angeles, she only came home to visit twice in fifty-three years. Hattie later married Cecil Sedberry, who was employed by the US Post Office for more than forty years. Cecil worked there until his retirement; he died in 1987. Hattie Mae died in California in 1999.

Inez Trigg Sanders, on the left, with her brother-in-law Chink Sanders and her sister-in-law Hattie Mae Sanders. The photograph was taken about 1946-1947 at a party to celebrate Chink Sanders's service in the United States Navy. Sanders family collection.

Chamberlin L. "Chink" Sanders, the third child and second son, graduated from I. M. Terrell in 1944, where he played football and ran track. Chink joined the navy in January 1946, and served on the troop transport ship USS *General W. A. Mann,* which brought soldiers back from Guam.[6] When he was released from naval service in late 1947, Chink returned home and enrolled in a trade school where he learned leather craft. He only used that training to do work like auto upholstery on a freelance basis and as a hobby. For most of his career, he worked at Universal Mills on North Beach Street (later Allied Mills) sewing sacks for grain and stock feed.[7] Chink's true passion, however, was baseball, and he played every day with dreams of becoming a major leaguer. He played semipro ball as a third baseman for the Grapevine Auctioneers of the North Texas Negro League, a team made up of players from Birdville, Riverside, Grapevine, and Mosier Valley. Chink Sanders followed in the footsteps of his older brother, A. J. "Buddy" Sanders, marrying Gladys Trigg, Inez's sister. The newlywed couple also lived with his parents, Edith and James Sanders, for a short time before buying land from Dollie Cheney and building their own house in the Garden of Eden.

Bernice and Lucinda Sanders, respectively the fifth and sixth of Edith and James's children, both graduated from I. M. Terrell High School in 1950. Lucinda, who was called "Lil Cindy," graduated with honors and went on to attend Prairie View A & M College, now Prairie View A & M University, a historically black school of higher education, located northwest of Houston. There she earned her bachelor's degree and a teaching certificate. Lucinda married Dan Russell, a fellow I. M. Terrell and Prairie View graduate. Dan joined the army as second lieutenant, and after he completed his service, the couple moved to Detroit, Michigan, where Dan worked for the transit system for more than thirty years. In Detroit, Lucinda earned a master's degree in education from Wayne State University and taught in the local school system for thirty years.

Music was an important part of family life in the Garden of Eden. In this 1955 photograph, Drew Sanders plays guitar for his mother, Inez, and his cousin Thomas Earl Sanders. Sanders family collection.

Like Lucinda, Bernice Sanders also earned good grades in school. She played bass fiddle in the I. M. Terrell High School orchestra and could also play piano and compose. One song, the "Alphabet Boogie," should have been recorded. It enabled the young students to say, or sing, the alphabet backward and forward. Bernice worked as a cook at the Haltom City Café as well as in other food service businesses. She married Floyd Jefferson and lived for a time in the Joe Louis Addition.

Dollie Sanders Gentry trained as a licensed vocational nurse at Harris Hospital before graduating from Texas Woman's University as a registered nurse. She specialized in the field of organ transplant procurement and is widely recognized for her expertise in facilitating African American organ donations. Sanders family collection.

Early on, James and Edith Sanders bought a piano so that the girls could learn to play. James taught himself to play the mandolin at an early age. Both before and after the children were born, relatives from both sides of their families would come down on weekends and play music all night. During those sessions, the Garden of Eden was a jumpin' place, and Bernice received both talent and training from each side of her family. Bernice became the first pianist for Valley Baptist Church. She had an emotionally difficult life, but Bernice's musical talent sustained her, and she lived well into her eighties.

Delbert Sanders, James and Edith's eighth child, graduated from I. M. Terrell High School in 1957, where he excelled in all varsity sports. He was a three-year starting quarterback for the football team, the Terrell Panthers; ran track, advancing to the state competition every year; and played both basketball and baseball. Not to be outdone in the music department, he played slide trombone during junior high school. Delbert was the first of James and Edith Sanders's children to receive a four-year college scholarship, to Tennessee Agricultural and Industrial

University in Nashville (renamed Tennessee State University in 1968). Instead of attending the university, however, Delbert decided to marry Beverly Tolliver, his high school sweetheart. Delbert was a talented woodworker employed by C&S Woodcrafters, a Fort Worth company that made furniture for hotels throughout the United States. He was promoted to a managerial position and worked with the company for more than thirty years. Beverly Sanders was the registrar for O. D. Wyatt High School in Fort Worth. Like most of the women in the Cheney and Sanders families, Beverly was a talented cook who made the best oatmeal cookies on earth. After Delbert and Beverly divorced, he later married Alicia Garcia. The marriage merged two cultures. Alicia, known as Lisa by the family, is known for her hot tamales and her Spanish translation skills.

Dollie Sanders, the ninth child who was named after her great aunt Dollie Cheney, was born at home in the Garden of Eden. She graduated from I. M. Terrell High School in 1958, where she played on the varsity volleyball team, served on the student council, was a member of the dance club, and played the B-flat clarinet in the senior band. Dollie was named both the school's "Most Studious Girl" and "Best Girl Athlete" for 1958. After graduation, Dollie married Henry Gentry, who was also an I. M. Terrell graduate. Henry was both a barber and a union carpenter. He worked for General Motors and owned Mud Masters, Incorporated, a general contracting business. After retirement, he ran a ranch in Navarro County. Dollie was one of the first African American employees at Harris Hospital, where she started as an elevator operator, and it sparked her love for the health-care field. She first obtained her licensed vocational nursing certificate from the Harris Hospital School of Nursing in 1963; once her children entered high school, she earned a Bachelor of Science degree in nursing from Texas Woman's University in Denton. After almost forty years with Harris Hospital, where she served as the renal transplant coordinator, Dollie Gentry began working for LifeGift as a coordinator for organ-transplant procurement. She is an acknowledged expert in the field of African American organ donation. Dollie Sanders Gentry was named a 2002 Healthcare Hero for her work educating families about the importance of organ donation, and in 2008 was honored with a Living Legend Award by the Renaissance Cultural Center.[8]

James McKinley "Dooney" Sanders Jr., who was named for his father but escaped the "Dick Cheney" nickname, was the tenth child and the last of the Sanders children born at home. He graduated from I. M. Terrell High School in 1959. Dooney was good at both academics and athletics. He was a catcher on the Terrell Panther's varsity baseball team, which won the state finals his senior year. Unfortunately, the team was disqualified as the champion team because of an ineligible player. Not surprisingly, his Terrell yearbook photo shows him wearing a letter jacket. Dooney learned to play the trumpet at Carver Junior High and became an accomplished musician. He formed his first band while still at Carver, with fellow students Walter Earl McDonald, Gerald Hardgraves, James Washington, Charles Hudson, and Joe Butler. They even recorded a record, with "Skinny Legs" on the A-side and "Juanita" on the flip. Keeping with the family's musical tradition, sometimes the band played on his parents' front porch on Saturday nights. Who knows what James and Edith Sanders thought of the tougher blues and rock and roll tunes?

Dooney formed an integrated band while he was in high school, and the group played a number of venues, including both African American and white clubs. The band's name changed over the years, starting with King James and the Rocking Teens (Dooney was King James, and the other band members were Junior Hunter, Dicky Pennerson, Ronnie Thayer, Jerry Anglin, and manager Curtis Cauthern—all white), followed by King James and the Galaxies, named after one member's 1959 Ford Galaxy (Clyde George, Raymond George, Lonnie "Brer" Saddler, and Joe Daniels). Then there was Jack and the Jivers (Tommy Lott,

Quincy Brown, and "Shoe Shine Red"). Dooney and his band played all over North Texas, and they were the first African American performers to appear at some of the venues.

Despite his love for music, Dooney continued to pursue his interest in baseball, playing semipro ball for the Fort Worth Comets, the Fort Worth Warriors, and the Grapevine Auctioneers. He took time from his musical and sporting interests to work for TXI, which had acquired Fort Worth Sand and Gravel, and for Harbison-Fischer. Dooney married Cessely Hogan, who worked for the Fort Worth Independent School District, in 1963. She played piano for the Sanders-Trigg Family Choir as well as for Valley Baptist Church.

Bob Ray Sanders probably has the highest public profile of any of James and Edith's children, due not only to his intellect and hard work but also because of changing values in the era of civil rights. Had he been born in 1923, like his oldest brother, instead of 1947, not as many doors would have been open to him, no matter how smart he was or how hard he worked. The baby of the family, he and his older brother Johnny Zero, who died shortly after birth, were the only two of the couple's twelve children born in a hospital. He was born "Bobby Ray," and that is how many members of his family still refer to him, but the shorter version of his name works better professionally. Bob Ray graduated from I. M. Terrell in 1965. He was president of the National Honor Society, played the B-flat clarinet in the senior band, and was the senior associate editor of the high school newspaper. Bob Ray was one of the first African American students at North Texas State University (now the University of North Texas), graduating with a bachelor's degree in journalism and a teaching certificate. He was the first African American to do his student teaching in the Birdville Independent School District, which was off-limits to black students until 1964.

Bob Ray Sanders never had to use his teaching certificate in the classroom, but many would argue that he has been educating the public

Bob Ray Sanders has not only had a significant career with the Fort Worth Star-Telegram *but also with KERA public television and radio. He helped start and was a reporter for the groundbreaking* Newsroom *program at KERA-TV and managed the KERA-FM radio station. Bob Ray is shown here at the microphone shortly after KERA-FM went on the air in 1974. Courtesy KERA.*

in North Texas in his role as a journalist. He began his career in 1969, writing for the *Fort Worth Star-Telegram*. Bob Ray moved to KERA in 1972, where he spent eighteen years in public broadcasting, hosting a radio show and serving as a reporter on the pioneering television news program, *Newsroom*. He also served as manager of the radio station KERA-FM for a number of years. Bob Ray turned down a number of offers to move to a national market and returned to the *Star-Telegram* as a columnist in 1994. He has won many awards, including multiple Press Club of Dallas Katie Awards, three Corporation for Public Broadcasting Awards, a first-place National Headliner Award for investigative reporting, a first-place award from the National Association of Black Journalists, a 2006 Dr. Marion J. Brooks Living Legend Award, and a regional Emmy Award.

Bob Ray married Dorothy Brown, who attended Texas Woman's

James and Edith Sanders celebrated their golden anniversary in 1972.
Sanders family collection.

University, where she received a degree in physical therapy. Dorothy works as a physical therapist, plays piano, is active in Links, and—befitting a member of the Cheney-Sanders family—is a gourmet cook. Journalism is not Bob Ray's only writing outlet, as he has also written poetry, plays, and a book about the Fort Worth photographer Calvin Littlejohn. Like other members of his family, he has musical interests as well—directing for both his church and the Sanders-Trigg Family Choir.

When the Civil Rights Bill was passed in 1964, a number of the public schools in Texas took steps toward integration. That same year, Julius Bussey, the principal of Haltom High School in the Birdville Independent School District, visited James, Edith, Buddy, and Inez Sanders before the school year began. Bussey had grown up with Buddy Sanders, and his own father, Tom Bussey, was a good friend of James Sanders. Anita Bussey, his wife, visited Edith Sanders on a regular basis, and the children of all three families played together.

Julius Bussey extended an invitation to the Sanderses, asking if they would be interested in allowing their children, Bob Ray and Drew, to become the first blacks to enroll at Haltom High School. Bob Ray, who was James and Edith's son, and Drew, who was Inez and Buddy's son, were both about to start their senior year at I. M. Terrell High School. After some thought, both young men declined the offer. Both preferred to attend Terrell and enjoy their senior year with friends they had known the entire time that they were in school. To miss that opportunity would have been devastating

The next fall, in 1965, two Sanders daughters made the jump to Haltom High School, the first members of the Cheney-Sanders family to attend an integrated high school. Brenda Sanders, who was Inez and Buddy's daughter, and Hattie Sanders, who was Gladys and Chink's oldest daughter, enrolled as juniors at Haltom High School. Brenda was a member of the National Honor Society, FHA, and the volleyball team, and Hattie was also a member of FHA. In 1967, Brenda and Hattie were the first blacks to graduate from Haltom High School.

CHAPTER 12

Rebuilding Community in the Twenty-first Century

Whats left of the Garden of Eden? Physically, the land holdings are much smaller than the two hundred acres Major Cheney and the Loyds owned at the turn of the twentieth century. When Major and Malinda Cheney sold a small piece of land to Fort Worth Sand and Gravel, it set off an industrial cascade that snowballed as small-scale family farms became less profitable. Most of the land Dollie Cheney inherited was sold during the 1930s and 1940s, passing permanently out of the family's control. Even James Sanders's sixty-or-so-acre holdings from the late 1930s are much reduced, either sold or given to other family members and then sold. To the untrained eye, the area looks like a patchwork of auto salvage lots, industrial warehouses, a church, vacant land, and a smattering of small homes.

The core of the Garden of Eden is intact. About fifteen acres, most of it fronting on Carson Street, have been owned by a member of the Cheney or Sanders family for better than 125 years. Although Major and Malinda Cheney's house burned in 1946, there are currently four houses left on the Cheney estate: Lucinda Johnson Sadler's house at 1420 Carson Street, the house at 1412 Carson Street formerly owned by Joe Marshall and Opal Trigg Woods (Opal was Inez and Gladys's sister), A. J. "Buddy" and Inez Trigg Sanders's house at 1408 Carson Street, and James and Edith Sanders's house at 1400 Carson Street. Dollie Cheney's house was demolished in the years after her death. There are also several parcels of vacant land still owned by the family. Some are farmed, while others await new structures, including a reconstruction of Major and Malinda Cheney's substantial home.

The true heart of the Garden of Eden is its people. This story is about how the Cheney and Sanders families worked to create a sense of place despite the harsh realities of everyday life. Jim Crow, early death due to accidents or illness, children who lashed out choosing alcohol and violence over hard work, limited professional opportunities for people of color, the Great Depression, encroaching industry that spoiled the Garden of Eden's buffer against the outside world, segregation—these realities made their life a tough hill to climb.

The pioneer family members who first came to Texas or who were born here before the Civil War ended were a determined lot. Both Green Loyd and Rush Loyd wisely maintained a strong relationship with the white Loyd family, whose ability to assist them grew with the white family's wealth. But they didn't take handouts. Green Loyd bought his own land, and Rush Loyd bought land in 1874, only nine years after the Civil War ended, and applied for and received a sizeable land grant. Although none of that land was in the Garden of Eden, it gave the family a firmer financial footing and the means to make a living. Both men were involved in civic affairs, registering to vote as soon as they were allowed to do so.

Major Cheney is, to some degree, a shadowy figure. Little can be confirmed about his early years, but it is clear that he had grit and determination. He assembled land holdings through purchases as well as by inheritance from Rush and Green Loyd—still no easy feat for a person of color in the decades following the Civil War. The man that emerged in the 1880s, following his marriage to Malinda Loyd, was a strong, no-nonsense character determined to carve out a safe haven for his family. Malinda Loyd Cheney, who was definitely born a slave, learned from her father and uncle, Green and Rush Loyd. She did not step outside the traditional role established for women in the nineteenth century, but focused her work on the home front. It was a time when a great deal of physical labor went into maintaining a household, and she did all of that work well and with a great deal of love. As it was with many families, Malinda Cheney was the glue that held the family together.

Neither Major nor Malinda could read or write, and they understood how that hampered their ability to succeed in an increasingly complex society. They knew that education would be the key to success for their children, and gave of their resources and time to establish a school for African American children. Even though all but one of their children died young, all who reached school age learned to read and write. Although segregation generally limited the Cheneys' children and grandchildren to more menial jobs, they understood the value of education. By the time great-grandchildren finished their schooling, they could take advantage of a new set of career opportunities—choosing, rather than settling for—a particular job. Early on, government and military careers provided the most reliable access to the middle class for people of color. Moving into more urban areas or out of Texas entirely offered broader opportunities as well. Several of the great-grandchildren left the Garden of Eden to settle in Fort Worth, other Texas cities, or other states.

The Sanders great-grandchildren and great-great-grandchildren chose careers in journalism, financial investments, teaching, law enforcement, preaching, dentistry, the postal service, nursing, banking, music and the arts, the military, sales, culinary arts, insurance, engineering, business, and medical technology. Others applied their skills as carpenters, auto mechanics, heavy equipment operators, personal trainers, secretaries, and—following in Major Cheney's footsteps—farming.

Dollie Cheney died in 1974, Major Guerry in 1975, and James

"Dick Cheney" Sanders in 1978, bringing to a close the two generations of children and grandchildren who had known both Major and Malinda well. Buddy Sanders was only two years old when his great-grandfather, Major Cheney, died, and eight years old when Malinda Cheney passed away. His younger siblings were either infants or had not been born when both Major and Malinda were still alive. Dollie Cheney, who had a story or a saying for almost every situation, recounted early life on the farm for anyone who would listen—and for some who tried not to. When she died, a major link with the Garden of Eden's past was gone.

The thread that kept the past alive was Sunday dinners after church. All family members, and quite a few guests, attended. Malinda Cheney's recipes graced the table along with dishes from Mama Edith (Edith Sanders), Mama 'Nez (Inez Trigg Sanders), Aunt Doll (Dollie Cheney), Aunt Cindy (Lucinda Johnson Sadler), Dollie Sanders Gentry, and others. There is nothing like slathering butter on a big slice of pecan pound cake or biting into a perfect piece of hot-water cornbread to stir talk about the women who regularly shared those delicacies with the family. Bob Ray Sanders also preserved family lore in his columns for the *Fort Worth Star-Telegram*. He remembered not only the love and care family members demonstrated for each other but also how they called a fool, a fool. Aunt Doll—Dollie Cheney—was particularly good at this, and her quips have remained relevant as appropriate retorts for tomfoolery or hateful language.

In 2004, Brenda Sanders-Wise, the oldest daughter of Buddy Sanders and Inez Trigg Sanders, moved back to the Garden of Eden with her husband, Dennis Wise, after retiring from a career with Merrill Lynch. Her career had taught her good financial and organizing skills. Although several family members had gathered genealogical records in preparation for a written history, Brenda was determined to raise the profile of the Garden of Eden. She rounded up family members and

A. J. "Buddy" Sanders and his wife, Inez Trigg Sanders, celebrated their fiftieth
wedding anniversary in 1994 with all of their living children present. From left
to right, the children are: Phillip R. Sanders, A. J. "Drew" Sanders, Brenda
Sanders-Wise, Trina Sanders, Chorlette Sanders Robinson, Timothy E.
Sanders, and Michaelangelo Antoine Sanders. Sanders family collection.

neighbors to establish the Garden of Eden Neighborhood Association
in 2004. She organized a Garden of Eden reunion in June of 2005, invit-
ing anyone who had lived in or had connections to the Garden of Eden
to the three-day event. There was at least one representative in attendance from of each of the fifty-four homes that once stood in either the
Garden of Eden or in the Joe Louis Addition.[1] They gathered stories

and recipes, swapped photographs and documents, and talked about how to tell the story of living on this chosen land.

Using the historical and genealogical information compiled by family members, Brenda and Trina Sanders wrote a historic district nomination that was submitted to Fort Worth's Historic and Cultural Landmarks Commission. The nomination discussed the strong, enduring cultural and family history of the neighborhood rather than focusing simply on architecture. The Carson Street Garden of Eden Historic and Cultural Landmark District was approved by members of the Fort Worth City Council in 2005, as the first African American historic district in Fort Worth. The goal of the designation is to preserve both the homes that remain in the Garden of Eden and the way of life that endured for many generations, while still allowing for redevelopment. The district guidelines state:

> The purpose of these guidelines is to discourage demolition of the District's historic buildings and cultural landmarks and to serve as a guide for rehabilitation of existing buildings, construction of new buildings and additions and relocation of buildings so as to preserve the historic and cultural character and the visual identity of the District. The purpose of design review is not to prohibit additions, new construction and other alterations, but to ensure that the overall integrity of the District is preserved.[2]

The guidelines also state that "agricultural gardening shall be permitted in the back and side yards to maintain the integrity of the period that the District is preserving."[3] The Garden of Eden is one of only eleven historic and cultural districts in Fort Worth, and its designation spurred local district designations in other historic African American neighborhoods, including Carver Heights, Terrell Heights, and Stop Six Sunrise Edition.

The Garden of Eden Neighborhood Association also coordinated the rehabilitation of a home in the Joe Louis Addition that belonged to Josephine Johnson. In 1996, Mrs. Johnson's sixty-one-year-old son, Herbert Johnson Jr., was senselessly shot and killed as he picked up trash in the front yard. The murder turned out to be a hate crime, perpetrated by a man who, with a friend, went out looking for a black person to kill. The murderer was sentenced to life in prison.[4] Mrs. Johnson was afraid and unable to return home after the shooting, so she went to live with her daughter. Ten years later, the ninety-three-year-old widow was ready to return to the home where she had raised her children, but the structure had deteriorated badly during her absence. The Garden of Eden Neighborhood Association arranged for Bruce Carter, a real estate investor, and Don Burse, a contractor, to repair the home at no cost to Mrs. Johnson. She was able to move back into her home in April 2006.[5]

A second project, started in 1999, was also completed in 2006. The historic New Trinity Cemetery, where many members of the Cheney, Sanders, and other Northeast Tarrant County African American families are buried, received a Texas Historic Cemetery Designation from the Texas Historical Commission. The cemetery is now marked with a Historic Texas Cemetery Medallion, and information about the size of the graveyard, its eight hundred known burials, and existing grave markers has been recorded for posterity and to protect the cemetery.[6]

All of these projects led to the Garden of Eden being selected as the 2006 Neighborhood of the Year at the Neighborhoods USA conference in Kansas City, Missouri. The Garden of Eden Neighborhood Association also won a first-place prize in the Social Revitalization/ Neighborliness category.[7] Former city council member Frank Moss noted, "They have worked hard to make sure that they aren't going to be a neighborhood that is going to disappear."[8]

Gathering the fruits of their labor at the Garden of Eden reunion, a committee that had always treasured the recipes handed down from family to family decided to publish a cookbook that would help to raise

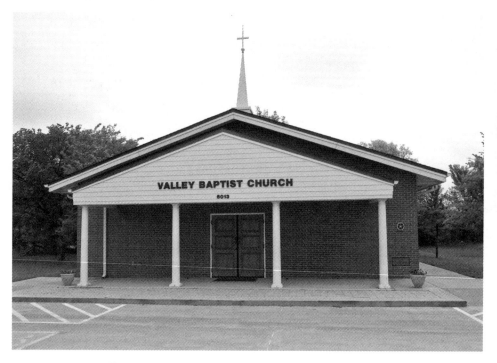

Valley Baptist Church as it was rebuilt following the tornado.
Hasson Diggs, photographer.

money to rebuild the Major and Malinda Cheney home and preserve the neighborhood's history. Those recipes—the backbone of Sunday dinners and holiday celebrations—were collected. Desserts held the starring role, and were featured in a "Christmas in the Garden of Eden" potluck dinner celebration held in December 2006, which also gathered additional recipes. *Recipes from Out to the House: Seasoned with Soul* was published in 2007 and has sold over five hundred copies.

April 13, 2007, which happened to be a Friday the thirteenth, almost spelled the end for the Garden of Eden. The weather was humid, and it was tornado season in North Texas. Things were quiet for most of the day. A bit after 6:00 p.m., a storm system moved across Northeast Tarrant County causing hail damage to twenty thousand homes and thirty thousand cars. A tornado swept through Haltom City and the Garden of Eden, packing a lot of punch for its relatively diminutive size. The winds were reportedly only 110 miles per hour, but the storm killed one man at a lumberyard in Haltom City, wiped out a row of homes south of State Highway 121 (in the 1937 white addition that was also called the Garden of Eden), and demolished the Valley Baptist Church on Elliott Reeder Road in the Garden of Eden.[9] The church was flattened, with no hope of repair.

The 1963 building stood on land that Dollie Cheney had sold to the church back in 1949, well before the first place of worship was built there in 1953. Like the homes in the Garden of Eden, Valley Baptist Church was a community center, and its destruction dealt the neighborhood not only a severe physical but a savage emotional blow. There was no question about rebuilding the church. It was central to the life and spirit of the community. Members went to work soliciting donations and assistance with plans and construction services. The old church building, with only 1,300 square feet of floor space, had been bursting at the seams. The new church facility cost $325,000 and contained 3,300 square feet of space, including seating for 209 people in the sanctuary, Sunday school classrooms, and a fellowship hall. Craig Stovall and the members of Fellowship Church in Grapevine worked with Drew Thigpen, Kelly Giddens, Roy Chumley, Jerome Stock of the Beck Group, and the membership of Valley Baptist to make the new church home a reality. The church was dedicated on November 22, 2009, a time of true Thanksgiving and rebirth for those who made their physical or spiritual homes in the Garden of Eden.[10] Amazingly, the church's baby grand piano, acquired just before the tornado hit, survived the storm with only a broken leg. It was restored and has a place of honor in the sanctuary, so that music, such an important part of life in the Garden of Eden, still reverberates when the piano's chords and the voices of the choir fill the air. In January 2010, Valley Baptist Church purchased a vacant lot adjacent to the church building from the heirs of C. L. "Chink" Sanders for future expansion plans. The success of the church-rebuilding program was wind in the sails for those working toward the rebirth of the Garden of Eden.

Education and the benefits it brought were one of the hallmarks of life in the Garden of Eden. Not only did Major and Malinda Cheney support the Birdville Colored School with their time and money, succeeding generations made sure that children received as much education as could be stuffed into them. They realized that the key to all understanding was education. Even when their children could not attend schools in Birdville or Haltom City, the families of the Garden of Eden maintained a working relationship, and sometimes a friendship, with people in those communities.

The longstanding educational contributions of the Cheney and Sanders families were not forgotten. In the summer of 2009, the Birdville Independent School District Board of Trustees voted to change the name of South Birdville Elementary to Major Cheney Elementary School at South Birdville, in memory of Major Cheney and the work he did to further educational opportunities for those living in South Birdville and the Garden of Eden.[11] Established in the early 1950s, the school was segregated until 1964, when Birdville ISD schools integrated. Several students from the Sanders family were finally able to attend a neighborhood school. The dedication ceremonies for the renamed school, held November 2, 2009, with dozens of family members in attendance, affirmed the family's enduring commitment to education.

After being moved from its initial location close to the Trinity River, Major and Malinda Cheney's home stood for over two decades at the corner of Carson Street and Elliott Reeder Road. When it burned in 1946, not only was the fifty-six-year-old house lost, but also many of the papers and photographs that documented the family's history. The house was emblematic of the full and vibrant life that this pocket of

Edenic land in the Trinity River bottoms provided for the extended family, away from the harsher realities of a segregated state. As current family members try to gather the stories and materials that are left, the absence of the Cheney house represents a great void in the story. The Garden of Eden Neighborhood Association has vowed to rebuild the house following the few documents and images that still exist, so that there will be a visible reminder of the world that Major and Malinda Cheney created. That won't rid the area of the nearby industrial uses, but it will help to establish a better sense of the original neighborhood. It may facilitate the reclamation of the land that made up the Cheney farm, but more importantly, it will preserve their story and ensure that succeeding generations know what a Garden of Eden their forbearers created.

Major Cheney Elementary School at South Birdville was named for Major Cheney in 2009, honoring his commitment to provide educational opportunities for his family and the African American community that lived in the area. Courtesy Birdville Independent School District.

The Sanders family gathered in a Garden of Eden back yard follow

...ster Sunday dinner in 2015. Hasson Diggs, photographer.

APPENDIX

Family Connections

This section presents a limited genealogy for the Loyd, Cheney, and Boaz families, both white and African American. The information on the white family lines (pp.168-169) shows not only Major Cheney's connection with the white branch of the Cheney family, but the frequency with which given names were shared in both the black and white sides of a family. The 1890s saw a number of marriages uniting the African American Cheney, Loyd, and Boaz families, not only with each other but with other families in communities outside the Garden of Eden. These marriages solidified and deepened the ties between the families.

The icon indicates a son or daughter of Malinda and Major Cheney.

Major and Malinda Cheney's Descendants

Major Cheney (1856-1925) + Malinda Loyd (1862-1931)
 Hattie Cheney (1885-1914) + James "Jimmy" Sanders (1883-1902)

        James McKinley "Dick Cheney" Sanders (1902-1978) + Edith M. Johnson (1904 -1979)

1) Andrew James "Buddy" Sanders (1923-1999) + Inez
   Trigg (1926-2002)
   > A. J. "Bubba" or "Drew" Jr.
   > Brenda
   > Paul (born/died 1950)
   > Chorlette
   > Phillip
   > Timothy
   > Trina
   > Michaelangelo Antoine

2) Hattie Mae Sanders (1925-1999) + Alwyn Sadler
   (1922 -2007)
   > Alwyn Jr.
   > + *Cecil C. Sedberry (1925-1987); no children*

3) Chamberlin L. "Chink" Sanders (1927- 1997)
   +Gladys Trigg (1930-   )
   > Hattie
   > Thomas Earl
   > Chamberlin L. "Lucky" Jr.
   > Bruce McKinley
   > + *Josephine High (1933-2001)*
   > *Curtis Mason (stepson)*

4) Chaney Sanders (1929-1995) + Lilly Rose Roberson
   (1932-2003)
   > Chanalene
   > Raymond Earl
   > + *Joan Holbert (1936-   )*
   > Chaney "Scrappy" Jr.

> Reginald "Reggie"
> Edith
> Cedric
> Thyra

5) Bernice Sanders (1931-2014) + Floyd Jefferson (1930-1974)
> Floretta Diana "Dinky"
> Tarvis
> Phillippa "Leapy"
> Paranell
> Ron
> Millie
> Tammulia "Tammy"
> Kareem "Slugger"

6) Virgil Lucinda "Lil Cindy" Sanders (1933-) + Dan M. Russell (1930-1993)
> Dan "Pooney" Jr.
> Patricia "Tweet"
> Lillette Michelle "Shelly"

7) Edward Sanders (1935- 1989) + Rosa Lee Bettis (1940-2014)
> Sharon
> James Edward
> LaQueta
> + *Rose Marie Byas*
> *Cassandra Smith (stepdaughter)*

8) Delbert Sanders (1937-) + Beverly Tolliver (1939-
1999)

       Michael

       Gerald

       Debra "Red"

       Leta Jo

       Delbert Jr.

  + *Alicia "Lisa" Garcia (1957-)*

       Daniel

       Arthur "Chano"

       Precilla

9) Dollie Sanders (1939-) + Henry L. Gentry Jr.
(1938-2006)

       Niphateria "Nip"

       Pamela "Pam"

       Henry III

10) James McKinley "Dooney" Sanders Jr. (1941-) +
Cessely Hogan (1945-)

       Orlando

       Jaquita "Jaqui"

11) Johnny Zero Sanders (born/died 1944)

12) Bob Ray Sanders (1947-) + Dorothy "Peaches"
Brown (1951-)

       Chandon

🌿 *[Hattie Cheney] + Charley James (c. 1888-1915); no children*

🌿 Mary Cheney (1886-1908) + John Guerry (1884-1965)

        Major Guerry (1908-1975) + Delilah "Lila" Mae

        Williams (1900-1994); no children

🌿 Dollie Cheney (1887-1974) + Raymond Dennis; no children

 +C. T. Thorpe (-); *no children*

🌿 Lon Cheney (1890-1918) + Ida May Barton; no children

🌿 Lan/Landen/John/ "Land Willie" Cheney (1893-1921) +

 Dessie Keith; no children

🌿 Polk Cheney (1894-1926) + Laura Gilbert (-1978); no

 children

🌿 McKinley Cheney (c.1896-c.1907); no children

Green and Charlotte Loyd's Children

Green Loyd (1833-1913) + Charlotte Schumaker (1845-1897)

    Henry Loyd (c. 1858-) + Missouri Stoval (-)

    Eliza "Liza" Loyd (c.1860-1914) + _____ Stevans (-)

    Julia Loyd (c. 1861-)

    Malinda Loyd (1862-1931) + Major Cheney

    Emma/Euma Loyd (c. 1866-)

    Lee Loyd (c. 1869-1913)

    Martin Loyd (c. 1869-) +Sarah _____

    Abe Loyd (1870-1938) + Mercedes "Mercie" Daily

Ida Loyd (1874- 1922) + George McClardy (1879-1961)
    Manda//Maude McClardy (c. 1892-)
    Minnie McClardy (c. 1894-)
    Spencer McClardy (1897-1969)
    Samantha McClardy Thomas (1899-1926)
    George McClardy Jr. (1902-1968) + Alice Lee Ruffin
    Nicholas McClardy (c. 1907-)
Mary Ann "Lollie" Loyd (1880-1960) + Wesley McClardy (-)
Dick Loyd (1884-1932) + Mollie _____

Rush and Hannah Loyd's Children

Rush Loyd (c. 1855-1900) + Hannah "Annie" Reed (c. 1856-)
    Oscar Loyd (-)
    Rush W. Loyd Jr. (1875-1911) + Laura Buckner (1878-)
        Harold W. Loyd (1899-)
    + *Sadie* _____ *(c.1878-)*

Ed and Aurelia Boaz's Children

Ed Boaz (1849-1917) + Aurelia Jane Hampton (c. 1856-)
    George W. Boaz (c. 1871-)
    Clysta A. Boaz (c. 1874-)

Cunard Boaz (c. 1876-   ) + Mehaley Turner (-   )

Copeland "Dennis" Boaz (1880-1952)

Clara Boaz (1883-1953) + Joe Wilson (1878-1963)

      Edward W. Wilson (1907-2000) + Nettie _____

      Ida Wilson (1909-1993)

      Joe F. Wilson Jr. (1918 -   ) + Bobbie/Bobby _____

Mary E. Boaz (c. 1885-   )

Sarah Boaz (c. 1887-1916) + Jimmy Johnson (- c. 1909/10)

      Edith "Mama Edith" Johnson (1904-1979) + James McKinley "Dick Cheney" Sanders (1902-1978) — see Cheney family for list of their children

      Lucinda "Aunt Cindy" Johnson (1907-2003) + Silas Robinson (1905-1961); no children

      +Hillman Sadler (1899-1974); no children

Amanda Robins Davis's Children

Amanda Robins (1866-1960) + Dr. Sanders (white)

    James "Jimmy" Sanders (1883-1902) + Hattie Cheney (1885-1914)

+ Jess Howard

    Jessie Howard (1886-1948)

      Frank Howard (1908-2007) + Senola Felder (1906 - 2002)

+ Mack Davis **(1859-1911)**

    Julius Davis (1890/1891-1975)

Annie Davis (c. 1892-   )
>   Johnnie B. Bell (1910-1981)
Mack Davis Jr. (1896-1960) + Bessie _____
Winnie Davis (1898-1976) + _____ White
Mollie Davis (1900-1965) + William Clayton
+ *Oscar Nichols*
Katie Bell Davis (1903-1989)
Warren Davis (1906-1978) + Emma Mae _____ (c. 1908-   )
Bennie Daggett Davis (1910-1961)

The White Cheney Family

John Cheney Sr. (1765-1838) + Rachel Benson Cheney (c. 1763-c.1801)

Aquilla Cheney (1785-1869)
Thomas Benson Cheney (1788-1845)
Julia Cheney (1790-1882)
Richard Cheney (1792-   )
Margaret Cheney (1794-   )
John Richard "Dick" Cheney Jr. (1796-1868) + Lucy Evans Owen
>   (1794-1836)
>   Mary O. Cheney (1817-   )
>   Lewis Rabon/Rayburn Cheney (1818-1889)
>   Dr. Francis Marion Cheney (1821-1874)

John G. Cheney (1828-1880) + Eliza J. Watts (c. 1839-1908)

John O. Cheney (1880-1925)

Catherine Cheney (c. 1866-   )

Alzada Cheney (c. 1872-   )

Dr. Jasper Newton Cheney (1832-1911) + Mary A. Preston

+ *Charlotte Shaw (c. 1815-1849)*

Arthur K. Polk Cheney (1847-1928)

William D. Cheney (1848-1851)

A. Jane Cheney (1849-1880)

+ *unidentified slave woman [not married]*

Major Cheney (1856-1925)

Samuel Cheney (1798-   )

Joseph Cheney (1801-1802)

[**John Cheney Sr.**]+ *Catherine Evans Owen (1781-1854)*

eight children, not related to this story

The White Loyd Family

Hale C. Loyd (1797-1871) + Rebecca W. Bottoms (1804-1877) [married 1822]

Dr. Thomas P. Loyd (1834-1868); no children

Martin Bottom "M. B." Loyd (1834-1912) + Margaret A. M. Valliant (1836-1895)

Ruth B. Loyd (1853-1913) + Samuel Burk Burnett
(1849-1922)
    Thomas Loyd Burnett (1871-1938) + Olive
    "Ollie" Lake (1871-1966)
        Ann Valliant Burnett (1900-1980)+
        Guy Waggoner
        + *James Goodwin Hall*
        + *Robert Windfohr*
        + *Charles Tandy*
    Frances Burnett (c.1874-1876)
    Anne Valliant Burnett (1876-1914) + F. E.
      Shoemaker (1854-   )
    +*Charles A. Johnson*

The White Boaz Family

Samuel Boaz (1809-1894) + Agnes Freeman (1818-1883)
    Hezekiah Boaz (1835-1861)
    Mary Frances Boaz (1836-1910)
    David Boaz (1838-1905)
    William Jesse "W. J." Boaz (1840-1916)
    Richard "Dick" Boaz (1843-1899)
    Elizabeth Sarah Boaz (1845-1925)
    Robert Leonidas Boaz (1855-1912)

NOTES

Introduction

1. Randolph B. Campbell, *An Empire for Slavery: The Peculiar Institution in Texas 1821-1865* (Baton Rouge: LSU Press, 1989), 11.
2. "Focus on Texas History: Colonization through Annexation," Center for American History, University of Texas at Austin, http://www.cah.utexas.edu/texashistory /annex/anglo (September 10, 2014).
3. "Census and Census Records," *Handbook of Texas Online*, http:// www.tshaonline.org/handbook/articles/ulc01, updated on June 12, 2010, published by the Texas State Historical Association (September 10, 2014).
4. Ibid.; Douglas Hales, "Free Blacks," *Handbook of Texas Online*, http:// www.tshaonline.org/handbook/online/articles/pkfbs, uploaded on June 12, 2010, published by the Texas State Historical Association (October 03, 2014).
5. "J. G. Cheney, deceased, Proof of Heirship," Tarrant County Deed Records, Vol. 291, 18, Tarrant County Clerk, Fort Worth, Texas.

Chapter 1: The Loyds and the Long Road to Texas

1. Alwyn Barr, *Black Texans: A History of African Americans in Texas, 1528-1995* (Norman: University of Oklahoma Press, 1996), 44.
2. "Colored Polls," Assessment of Poll Tax, in the County of Tarrant, for 1867, Tarrant County Tax Rolls 1850-1910, Reel 1, Texas State Library and Archives Commission.
3. "Green Lloyd [sic]," 1870 United States Census, www.FamilySearch.org/pal: /MM9.1.1/MXGD-M5C (January 16, 2012).
4. "Main Street Shooting," *Fort Worth Daily Gazette*, Vol. 14 No. 169, March 30, 1890, 7.
5. Mayes, also sometimes spelled Mays, was M. B. Loyd's nephew and lived with him as a young man. He was born in 1860, so it is unlikely that he was the actual slaveholder. The fact that Green Loyd lived next door to Hale and Rebecca Loyd and the record of Hale Loyd's slave holdings make it much more likely that he owned Green Loyd. Mayes appears in the photograph of the First National Bank staff.
6. "Marriage certificate for Hale Loyd and Rebecca Bottom," Image number 004705531, Kentucky County Marriages 1797-1954, www.FamilySearch.org

Notes

(March 5, 2013).

7. "A Brief History of Chickasaw County, Mississippi," Chickasaw County Historical and Genealogical Society, www.chickasawcountyhistorical.com (April 28, 2013).

8. John Leffler, "Palo Pinto County," Handbook of Texas Online, http://www.tshaonline.org/handbook/online/articles/hcp01, uploaded on June 15, 2010, published by the Texas State Historical Association (April 21, 2013).

9. "Capt. Loyd, 77, Texas Pioneer Banker, Dies," *Fort Worth Star Telegram*, April 16, 1912, 1.

10. David Paul Smith, *Frontier Defense in the Civil War: Texas' Rangers and Rebels* (College Station: Texas A&M University Press, 1992), 42. The militia or Texas Ranger group evolved and had different names throughout the Civil War. It was also called the Frontier Organization.

11. "M. B. Loyd," Texas, Muster Roll Index Cards - 1838-1900, Texas State Library & Archives Commission, http://interactive.ancestry.com/2059/32622_1020703347_0015-00442/34319?backurl=http%3a%2f%2fsearch.ancestry.com%2fcgi-bin%2fsse.dll%3findiv%3d1%26db%3dTexasMusterRollCards%26rank%3d1%26new%3d1%26MSAV%3d1%26msT%3d1%26gss%3dangs-d%26gsfn%3dm%2bb%2b%26gsln%3dlloyd%26uidh%3dy53%26pcat%3d39%26fh%3d5%26h%3d34319%26recoff%3d7%2b8%2b9%26ml_rpos%3d6&ssrc=&backlabel=ReturnRecord#?imageId=32622_1020703347_0015-00442 (November 3, 2012).

12. Smith, *Frontier Defense*, 94.

13. "M. B. Lloyd," Texas, Muster Roll Index Cards - 1838-1900, Texas State Library & Archives Commission http://interactive.ancestry.com/2059/32622_1220701439_0020-00998/60794?backurl=http%3a%2f%2fsearch.ancestry.com%2fcgi-bin%2fsse.dll%3findiv%3d1%26db%3dTexasMusterRollCards%26rank%3d1%26new%3d1%26MSAV%3d1%26msT%3d1%26gss%3dangs-d%26gsfn%3dm%2bb%2b%26gsln%3dlloyd%26uidh%3dy53%26pcat%3d39%26fh%3d0%26h%3d60794%26recoff%3d7%2b8%2b9%26ml_rpos%3d1&ssrc=&backlabel=ReturnRecord (November 3,2012).

14. "G. W. Loyd," Texas, Muster Roll Index Cards - 1838-1900, Texas State Library & Archives Commission, http://interactive.ancestry.com/2059/32622_1020703347_0015-00422/34294?backurl=http%3a%2f%2fsearch.ancestry.com%2fcgi-bin%2fsse.dll%3findiv%3d1%26db%3dTexasMusterRollCards%26rank%3d1%26new%3d1%26MSAV%3d1%26gss%3dangs-d%26gsfn%3dg.%2bw.%26gsln%3dlloyd%26uidh%3dy53%26pcat%3d39%26fh%3d1%26h%3d34294%26recoff%3d7%2b8%2b9%26ml_rpos%3d2&ssrc=&backlabel=ReturnRecord (November 2,

173

2012).

15. Smith, *Frontier Defense*, 54.

16. Robert Dunnam, "Frontier Regiment," *Handbook of Texas Online*, http://www
.tshaonline.org/handbook/online/articles/qjf01, uploaded on June 12, 2010,
published by the Texas State Historical Association (May 01, 2013).

17. Anonymous, *"Officers and Force of First National Bank, Fort Worth,"* photograph,
n.d. [before 1912], Photograph Collection, University of Texas at San Antonio, Accession number 81-0726.

18. "M. B. Loyd," Co. E, McCord's Frontier Regt Texas Cavalry, www.fold3.com (April
3, 2013).

19. "Malinda Chaney [sic]," Texas, Deaths, 1890-1976, *FamilySearch*, https://family-
search.org/pal:/MM9.1.1/K33Q-KWX (March 15, 2011).

20. "Loyd family marker, Oakwood Cemetery," *Find A Grave*, http://www.finda-
grave.com/cgi-bin/fg.cgi?page=gr&GRid=18747637 (March 5, 2013).

21. Julia Kathryn Garrett, *Fort Worth: A Frontier Triumph* (Austin: Encino Press, 1972),
260. Reprinted with a foreword by Jenkins Garrett and an index. Fort Worth: TCU
Press, 1996.

22. "M.B. Loyd," 1873 Tarrant County Tax Rolls, Texas State Library and Archives
Commission.

23. "Green Loyd," 1871 Tarrant County Tax Roll, Texas State Library and Archives
Commission; "Inflation Calculator," http://www.davemanuel.com/inflation-calcu-
lator.php (March 12,2013).

24. "M. B. Loyd," 1872 Tarrant County Tax Rolls, Texas State Library and Archives
Commission.

25. "J.M. Knight to Green Loyd," Tarrant County Deed Records, Vol. 50, 637, Tarrant
County Courthouse, Fort Worth, Texas, filed for record on February 10, 1888.

Chapter 2: Navidad Nation: The Cheney Family
in Lavaca County

1. "John Cheney," 1850 United States Census, Lavaca County, Texas, http://inter-
active.ancestry.com/8054/4206179_00191/1041924?backurl=http%3a%2f%2fsea
rch.ancestry.com%2fcgi-bin%2fsse.dll%3findiv%3d1%26db%3d1850usfedce-
nancestry%26rank%3d1%26new%3d1%26MSAV%3d1%26msT%3d1%26gss%3
dangsd%26gsfn%3djohn%26gsln%3dcheney%26msrpn__ftp%3dLavaca%2bCo
unty%252c%2bTexas%252c%2bUSA%26msrpn%3d1702%26msrpn_PInfo%3d7
%257c0%257c1652393%257c0%257c2%257c3249%257c46%257c0%257c1702

%257c0%257c0%257c%26uidh%3dy53%26_83004003n_xcl%3df%26pcat%3d3
5%26fh%3d0%26h%3d1041924%26recoff%3d%26ml_rpos%3d1&ssrc=&back-
label=ReturnRecord#?imageId=4206179_00191 (July 15,2013).

2. "John Cheney," Clerk Returns, Colorado County, Texas 1 & 2 Class, April 27, 1838, 1. This document lists land grants and either gives the date the person immigrated to Texas or states that the person was in Texas prior to May 2, 1835. John Cheney immigrated to Texas before May 2, 1835. Lavaca was created out of Colorado County in 1846.

3. "Indian Removal," *Encyclopedia of Oklahoma History & Culture*, http://digital.library.okstate.edu/encyclopedia/entries/I/IN015.html (April 23, 2014).

4. Paul Boethel, *History of Lavaca County*, rev. ed. (Austin: Von Boeckmann-Jones, 1959), 19.

5. John Cheney, 1st Class Colorado County, One League, Filed May 17, 1838, Patented June 10, 1841, General Land Office records, Colorado County, File 42, Ab103; John Cheney, 1st Class Colorado County, One Labor, Filed May 16, 1839, Patented June 10, 1841, General Land Office records, Colorado County, File 25, Ab13b,http://www.glo.texas.gov/ncu/SCANDOCS/archives_webfiles/arcmaps/web files/landgrants/PDFs/1/0/6/0/1060780.pdf (April 23, 2014).

6. Lewis R. Cheney, First Class Colorado County Land Grant, One-third League, Filed August 28, 1838, Patented June 12, 1841, General Land Office records, Colorado County, File 20, Ab 137; F. M. Cheney, Third Class Colorado County Land Grant, 320 acres, Filed June 1839, Clerk Returns Colorado County, Texas General Land Office records, Number 30; F. M. Cheney, Third Class Colorado County Land Grant, 160 acres, Filed May 20, 1838, Patented October 4, 1840, General Land Office records, Colorado County, File 104, Ab 125. The land described here is in Lavaca County, which split off from Colorado County in 1846, so these earlier records were filed in Colorado County.

7. Doug Kubicek, interview by Carol Roark, June 14, 2013; Christopher Long, "Lavaca County," *Handbook of Texas Online*, http://www.tshaonline.org/handbook/online/articles/hcl05, uploaded on June 15, 2010, published by the Texas State Historical Association (April 23, 2014); "Adeline Cunningham," interview in *Born into Slavery: Slave Narratives from the Federal Writers Project, 1936-1938*. Ex-Slave Stories (Texas), Vol. XVI, Part 1, *American Memory*, http://memory.loc.gov/cgi-bin/ampage?collId=mesn&fileName=161/mesn161.db&recNum=272&itemLink=r%3Fammem%2Fmesnbib%3A@field%28DOCID%2B@lit%28mesn%2F161%2F270263%29%29, (June 6, 2014).

8. Ibid., Kubicek.

9. "Slave Schedules," 1860 US Federal Census, Lavaca County, http://search.an-cestry.com/cgibin/sse.dll?db=1860slaveschedules&rank=1&new=1&so=3&MSA V=1&gss=ms_r_db&msrpn__ftp=Lavaca+County%2C+Texas%2C+USA&msrp n=1702&msrpn_PInfo=7%7C0%7C1652393%7C0%7C2%7C3249%7C46%7C 0%7C1702%7C0%7C0%7C&msrpn_x=XO&msrpn__ftp_x=1&dbOnly=_F000 29F2%2C2%7C_F00029F2%2C2_x&uidh=y53, (April 23, 2014).

10. The problem is that Major Cheney should appear as a member of the Cheney household in the 1860 US Federal Census records. He is neither listed as a free person on the regular census results nor as a slave owned by a member of the Cheney family on the slave schedules. Family accounts are very clear about his status as a free person of color, however, and the records from that time period may not have been entirely accurate, particularly for a child whose status the father was not interested in putting in the public record.

11. Bruce Glasrud, "Jim Crow's Emergence in Texas," *American Studies*. 15 (1974): 49.

12. "John G. Cheney," Texas, Muster Roll Index Cards - 1838-1900, Texas State Library & Archives Commission, http://search.ancestry.com/cgibin/sse.dll?indiv=1&db=TexasMusterRollCards&r ank=1&new=1&MSAV=1&msT=1&gss=angs-d&gsfn=john+g&gsln=ch-eney&uidh=y53&pcat=39&fh=0&h=107417&recoff=7+8+9&ml_rpos=1, (February 14, 2014); "John G. Cheney." United States Civil War Solders Index, 1861-1865, https://familyserach.org/pal:/MM9.1.1/F9K5-NZ6, (February 13, 2014).

13. John Gorman, "Reconstruction Violence in the Lower Brazos Valley," in *Still the Arena of Civil War: Violence and Turmoil in Reconstruction Texas*, ed. Kenneth W. Howell (Denton: University of North Texas Press, 2012), 387.

14. W. H. Heistead to Gen. Kiddo, January 24, 1867, Barry Crouch Collection, Victoria College, Box 4B, quoted in Douglas Kubicek and Carroll Scogin-Brinfield, "An Uncompromising Line between Yankee Rule and Rebel Rowdies: Reconstruction Violence in Lavaca County," in *Still the Arena of Civil War: Violence and Turmoil in Reconstruction Texas*, ed. Kenneth W. Howell (Denton: University of North Texas Press, 2012), 374.

15. Ibid., 371 and 377.

16. "Vienna (Cheney Settlement)" Texas Historical Marker. Historic Sites Atlas database. http://atlas.thc.state.tx.us/shell-site.htm (January 4, 2015).

17. Kubicek and Scogin-Brinfield, 378.

Chapter 3: Birdville: Setting the Stage for the
Garden of Eden

1. "Samuel Boaz," 1850 US Census, Slave Schedules, https://familysearch.org/pal:/MM9.1.1/MVZS-LTP (February 14, 2014).
2. "M Loyd slaves," 1860 US Census, Slave Schedules, http://search.ancestry.com /cgi-bin/sse.dll?db=1860slaveschedules&rank=1&new=1&so=3&MSAV =1&msT=1&gss=ms_r_db&gsfn_x=NP_NN_NIC&gsln=loyd&gsln_x=NN &msrpn__ftp=Palo+Pinto+County%2C+Texas%2C+USA&msrpn=2286 &msrpn_PInfo=7-%7C0%7C1652393%7C0%7C2%7C3249%7C46%7C0 %7C2286%7C0%7C0%7C&dbOnly=_F00029F2%7C_F00029F2_x&uidh =y53 (February 14, 2014).
3. "The Birdville Union has a good article on the resources of Texas," *Texas State Gazette* (Austin), January 1, 1859.
4. Ibid.
5. Eyvonne Andrews Eddins, Betty Porter and David Vorhees, *Birdville, Texas: Frontier Wilderness, County Seat, & Beyond* (Haltom City, TX: Birdville Historical Society, 2005), 13-15.
6. Brian Hart, "Birdville, TX," *Handbook of Texas Online,* http://www.tshaonline.org/handbook/online/articles/hrb34, uploaded on June 12, 2010, published by the Texas State Historical Association (March 24, 2014).
7. "Birdville, First County Seat, Joins Haltom City," *Fort Worth Star-Telegram*, July 7, 1949, 18.
8. *Birdville, Texas*, 26-27.
9. Kristi Strickland, "Barkley, Benjamin Franklin," *Handbook of Texas Online*, http://www.tshaonline.org/handbook/online/articles/fba67, uploaded on June 12, 2010, published by the Texas State Historical Association (March 23, 2014).
10. Gussie Scott Chaney, "Was Dallas Woman First Postmistress in United States?" *Dallas Morning News*, March 27, 1921, magazine section, 1.
11. "Barkley Funeral set for Thursday," *Dallas Morning News*, November 22, 1928, Sect. 2, 25.
12. "Sarah Boaz," 1910 US Census, http://search.ancestry.com/cgi-bin/sse.dll ?indiv=1&db=1910USCenIndex&rank=1&new=1&MSAV=1&msT=1&gss =angsd&gsfn=sarah&gsfn_x=NP_NN_NIC&gsln=boaz&gsln_x=NN &msrpn__ftp=Fort+Worth%2c+Tarrant%2c+Texas%2c+USA&msrpn =78432&msrpn_PInfo=8%7c0%7c1652393%7c0%7c2%7c3249%7c46%7c0 %7c2858%7c78432%7c0%7c&dbOnly=_83004006%7c_83004006_x%2c

_83004005%7c_83004005_x&uidh=y53&mscng0=edith&pcat=35&fh=0
&h=28596318&recoff=&ml_rpos=1 (June 6, 2014). The 1910 census lists Sarah
Boaz as a widowed head of household with two children, Edith Shanon and Lucinda Johnson. The different last names in the census record suggest that a suspicion the family held for many years might be true. The two girls looked very
different, and the family wondered if they might have had different fathers.
There seem to be no other records that confirm or deny this suspicion, and
Edith always used the Johnson surname before she married James "Dick
Cheney" Sanders.

13. "Hale Loyd," Find A Grave, http://www.findagrave.com/cgi-
bin/fg.cgi?page=gr&GRid=8889265&FLid=22081019& (June 6, 2014).

14. "Green Lloyd [sic]," 1871 Tarrant County Tax Roll, *Tarrant County Tax Rolls,
1846-1910*, Texas State Library & Archives Commission.

15. "Rush Lloyd [sic]," 1870 US Census, http://search.ancestry.com/cgi-bin/sse.dll
?indiv=1&db=1870usfedcen&rank=1&new=1&MSAV=1&msT=1&gss
=angsd&gsfn=rush&gsfn_x=NP_NN_NIC&gsln=loyd&gsln_x=NN&msrpn
__ftp=Tarrant+County%2c+Texas%2c+USA&msrpn=2858&msrpn_PInfo=7-
%7c0%7c1652393%7c0%7c2%7c3249%7c46%7c0%7c2858%7c0%7c0%7c&ui
dh=y53&pcat=35&fh=3&h=14594686&recoff=&ml_rpos=4 (March 12, 2014).

16. "Rush Loyd 160 acres," Robertson Preemption Grant, October 2, 1877, Tarrant
County, http://www.glo.texas.gov/ncu/SCANDOCS/archives_webfiles/ar-
cmaps/webfiles/landgrants/PDFs/3/4/0/340738.pdf (November 26, 2014).

17. Gregory A. Boyd, ed., *Texas Land Survey Maps for Tarrant County, With Roads,
Railways, Waterways, Towns, Cemeteries & Cross-referenced Indexes from the Texas
Railroad Commission and General Land Office* (Norman, OK: Arphax Publishing
Co., 2008), 162-163, 178-179.

18. "Rush and Hannah Loyd to Jeremiah Stewart," Tarrant County Deed Records.
Vol. O, 412.

19. "Green Loyd," 1876 Tarrant County Tax Roll, *Tarrant County Tax Rolls, 1846-
1910*, Texas State Library & Archives Commission.

20. *"Fort Worth, Texas* [map], 1885, scale not given, Texas Digital Sanborn Maps
1867-1970, http://sanborn.umi.com/image/view?state=tx&reelid= reel15
&lcid=8530&imagename=00006&mapname=Ft. Worth Feb 1885, Sheet
6&CCSI=514n, sheet 6, (June 4, 2014).

21. "Real Estate Transfers," *Dallas Morning News*, June 1, 1893, 5; Chris Cravens,
"Chicago, Rock Island and Texas Railway," *Handbook of Texas Online*,

http://www.tshaonline.org/handbook/online/articles/eqcaw, uploaded on June 12, 2010, published by the Texas State Historical Association (June 5, 2014).

22. "Real Estate Transfers," *Dallas Morning News*, October 2, 1894, 7.

23 The newspaper articles do not give Mrs. Bowman's first name, but the 1880 US Federal Census seems to indicate that her full name was Martha E. Bowman. Although she apparently moved soon after the attack, Martha E. Bowman was the right age and race and was a widow. She also had one son about the age of the boy described in the newspaper article.

24. "W. P. Thomas," 1880 US Census, http://search.ancestry.com/cgibin/sse.dll? indiv= 1&db=1880usfedcen&rank=1&new=1&MSAV=1&msT=1&gss=angs-d&gsfn=w+p&gsfn_x=NP_NN_NIC&gsln=thomas&gsln_x=NN&msrpn__ftp= Fort+Worth%2c+Tarrant%2c+Texas%2c+USA&msrpn=78432&msrpn_PInfo=8 %7c0%7c1652393%7c0%7c2%7c3249%7c46%7c0%7c2858%7c78432%7c0%7c &dbOnly=_F000686E%7c_F000686E_x%2c_83004006%7c_83004006_x%2c_ 83004005%7c_83004005_x&_83004002=white&uidh=y53&_83004003-n_xcl=f&pcat=35&fh=0&h=11643422&recoff=&ml_rpos=1. The census record shows that W. P. Thomas was a "City Policeman." Fort Worth City Directories published during this time period also show only one person named Thomas who was a police officer. That person was Walter P. Thomas.

25. "Ravished!" *Fort Worth Daily Democrat*, September 5, 1879, 4. Mrs. Bowman's neighbor was C. M. Bloodgood, not Bloodville, as indicated in the newspaper article.

26. "More About the Rape Case," *Fort Worth Daily Democrat*, September 7, 1879, 4.

27. "Old Jail Recalls Early Day History," *Fort Worth Telegram*, December 4 1904, 3.

28. "Rush Loyd Smuggled Off to Dallas," *Fort Worth Daily Democrat*, September 9, 1879, 4.

29. The State of Texas vs. Rush Loyd, Tarrant County Court Minute Book, March 11, 1880. v. C, 136.

30. The State of Texas vs. Rush Loyd, Tarrant County Court Minute Book, October 27, 1880. v. C, 571; "Tarrant County's Executions," *Fort Worth Star-Telegram*, August 15, 1909, 2.

Chapter 4: Aunt Doll and the Sam Bass Stories: Major Cheney Comes of Age

1. "Manerva and John Boone to John G. Cheney," Tarrant County Deed Records.

Vol. P, 549-551.

2. "Bass Bagged," *Denison Daily News*, July 23, 1878, 1; "Murphy the Spy," *Denison Daily News*, July 26, 1878, 1.

3 Helena Huntington Smith. "Sam Bass and the Myth Machine," *The American West*. Jan. 1970: 35.

Chapter 5: Early Life in the Garden of Eden

1. "John G. Cheney," 1880, Tarrant County Texas, US *Federal Census Mortality Schedules, 1850-1885*, http://search.ancestry.com/cgibin/sse.dll?indiv=1 &db=USMortality&rank=1&new=1&MSAV=1&msT=1&gss=angs-d&gsfn =john&gsfn_x=NP_NN_NIC&gsln=cheney&gsln_x=NN&msddy=1880 &msypn__ftp=Tarrant+County%2c+Texas%2c+USA&msypn=2858&msypn _PInfo=7%7c0%7c1652393%7c0%7c2%7c3249%7c46%7c0%7c2858%7c0 %7c0%7c&dbOnly=_F0007034%7c_F0007034_x%2c_83004005%7c _83004005_x&_83004002=white&uidh=y53&_83004003n_xcl=f&pcat =35&fh=0&h=123541&recoff=6+8+19+21&ml_rpos=1 (September 12, 2013). Cheney's middle initial has been mistranscribed as an "F." The original manuscript copy shows a "G." In addition, the 1880 US Census for Tarrant County also lists "Eliza J. Chaney" as a widow.

2. "Eliza J. Cheney," 1880 US Census, http://search.ancestry.com/cgi-bin/sse.dll?indiv=1&db=1880usfedcen&rank=1&new=1&MSAV=1&gss=angs-d&gsfn=eliza&gsfn_x=NP_NN_NIC&gsln=cheney&gsln_x=NN&msrpn__ftp= Tarrant+County%2c+Texas%2c+USA&msrpn=2858&msrpn_PInfo=7%7c0%7c 1652393%7c0%7c2%7c3249%7c46%7c0%7c2858%7c0%7c0%7c&dbOnly=_F 000686E%7c_F000686E_x%2c_83004006%7c_83004006_x%2c_83004005%7c _83004005_x&_83004002=white&uidh=y53&_83004003-n_xcl=m&pcat=35&fh=0&h=7287390&recoff=&ml_rpos=1 (March 14, 2014).

3. Bruce Glasrud, "Jim Crow's Emergence in Texas," *American Studies* 15 (1974): 50-51.

4. "Maj Chaney, col'd," 1882 Tarrant County Tax Roll, *Tarrant County Tax Rolls, 1846-1910*, Texas State Library & Archives Commission.

5. "Landon Booth and M. J. Booth to Major Cheney," Tarrant County Substitute Deed Record, Vol. 64, 467. This land was formerly owned by Simcoe Popplewell.

6. "Landon Booth to Major Cheney," Tarrant County Deed Records, Vol. 60, 395. Major Cheney also farmed on the land owned by Rush Loyd, both before and after Loyd's death.

7. Andrew J. "Buddy" Sanders drew the map showing the house and garden reproduced on page 47. It depicts the house after it was moved to Carson Street.

8. "This Beloved Recipe Takes the Cake," *Fort Worth Star-Telegram*, January 4, 2006, 2E.

Chapter 6: Other African American Communities in Tarrant County and How They Relate to the Garden of Eden

1. George N. Green, "Mosier Valley, TX," *Handbook of Texas Online*, http://www.tshaonline.org/handbook/online/articles/hrmud, uploaded on June 15, 2010, published by the Texas State Historical Association (June 9, 2014).
2. "Despite Changes Community Maintains Settlers' Heritage," *Fort Worth Star-Telegram*, August 1, 1991, 1.
3. "Amanda Davis," *Texas, Death Certificates, 1903–1982*, http://search.ancestry.com/cgi-bin/sse.dll?indiv=1&db=txdeathcerts&rank =1&new=1&MSAV=1&msT=1&gss=angsd&gsfn=amanda&gsfn_x=NP_NN _NIC&gsln=davis&gsln_x=NN&msddy=1960&msrpn__ftp=tarrant+county %2c+texas&_83004002=black&uidh=y53&_83004003n_xcl=m&pcat=34 &fh=0&h=22850644&recoff=9+10+21&ml_rpos=1 (June 6, 2014).
4. Amanda Davis and Maudy Davis 1900 US Census; Amanda Davis and Maudy Davis 1910 US Census; Katie Bell Davis Holloway Memorial Program. Mayfield Baptist Church, August 26, 1989, Drew Sanders Collection.
5. "Hattie Cheney and Jimmy Sanders," Wedding Certificate 10767, Tarrant County, Texas. Filed December 21, 1901.
6. "Frank Howard," *Fort Worth Star-Telegram*, November 4, 2007, B7.
7. Celebration of Life for Mrs. Johnnie B. Bell. Mayfield Missionary Baptist Church, December 5, 1981, Drew Sanders Collection.
8. "Our History," The Corinth Family [Corinth Baptist Church], http://www.thecorinthfamily.org/our_history.html (June 9, 2014).
9. Ibid.
10. "Riverside Colored Public School," *Tarrant County Historic Resources Survey Fort Worth: Upper North, Northeast, East, Far South, and Far West* (Fort Worth: Historic Preservation Council, 1989), 67.
11. Green Loyd to Tarrant County, right-of-way donation, December 4, 1888, Tarrant County Deed Records, Vol. 5, 206.
12. http://www.birdvillehistory.org/page7.php?aa=0&si0=6&si1=0&si2=0 (June 12, 2014).
13. Brian Hart, "Dove, TX," *Handbook of Texas Online*, http://www.tshaonline.org/handbook/online/articles/hvd35, uploaded on June 12, 2010, published by the Texas State Historical Association (June 14, 2014).
14. Leslie Hueholt, "Southlake Woman says Fleeing Slaves Stayed at Cave," *Fort*

Worth Star-Telegram, September 13, 1996, Northeast AM Section, 1.

15. Charles Young, "Bob Jones Eulogy - December 1936," *Southlake Journal*, September 15, 2006. This newspaper clipping is in the collections of the Southlake Historical Society.

16. Ibid.; "Wealthy Negro's Funeral Attended by White Friends," unknown newspaper, December 28, 1936.This newspaper clipping is in the collection of the Southlake Historical Society.

17. Adrienne Nettles, "Savvy Rancher a Pioneer Leader," *Fort Worth Star-Telegram*, February 14, 2008, B2.

18. Listings for the Dove, Texas, community, 1910 US Census.

19. "Black History Month," *Fort Worth Star-Telegram*, February 3, 1993, Metro, 21.

20. http://www.grapevinehistory.org/areahistory.html (June 15, 2014).

21. Ibid.; Sim Wright, Standard Certificate of Death, State of Texas, Texas Department of Health, Bureau of Vital Statistics, certificate number 5242, filed January 30, 1937.

Chapter 7: The Cheney Children

1.   Thelma Ray, *The History of Birdville* (Fort Worth: By the author, 1965), 79.

2.   "Birdville Colored School Teachers 1888-1906," list prepared by the Billy W. Sills Center for Archives, Fort Worth Independent School District, Fort Worth, Texas.

3.   "Mage Cheney and wife Malinda Cheney to W. D. Harris, County Judge of Tarrant County," Tarrant County Deed Records, Vol. 81, 526, Tarrant County Clerk, Fort Worth, Texas.

4.   Birdville Colored School Teachers.

5.   Ibid.

6.   "County School Trustees," Dallas Morning News, February 27, 1902, 7; "Tarrant County School Trustees," *Dallas Morning News*, May 14, 1903, 7.

7.   Standard Certificate of Death for "Lonnie Chaney [sic] Certificate number 9456, 11 February 1918," Death Certificates, Texas State Board of Health, Bureau of Vital Statistics.

8.   "Texas Death Certificate for Land Willie Chaney [sic], certificate number 8887, March 24, 1921," Texas Death Certificates, 1903-1982, http://interactive.ancestry.com/2272/33154_B06187800399/30043650?backurl=http%3a%2f%2fsearch.ancestry.com%2fcgibin%2fsse.dll%3findiv%3dtry%26db%3dtxdeathcerts%26h%3d30043650&ssrc=&backlabel=ReturnRecord (October 25, 2012).

9.   Mittie Coleman, interview with the author, March 24, 1976.

10. "22 Negroes are Selected by Two City Draft Boards," *Fort Worth Star-Telegram*,

October 28, 1917, Sect. 2, 6.

11. Nun Fretwell, interview with the author, July 16, 1981.

12. "Colored Delegates," *Fort Worth Morning Register*, October 14, 1899, 5.

13. "In the Courts," *Fort Worth Star-Telegram*, January 28, 1904, 3.

14. "Major Chaney [sic] vs Armour & Co., et. al.," Tarrant County 17th Civil District Court Records, Vol. A-6, 38, Tarrant County Clerk, Fort Worth, Texas.

15. Hattie and Lillie Hooper, interview with the author, October 21, 1980.

16. "Certificate of Death for James McKinley Sanders, certificate number 48105, June 22, 1978," Texas Death Certificates 1903-1982, http://search.ancestry.com/cgibin/sse.dll?rank=1&new=1&tid=46538852&tpid= 25101594131&ssrc=pt_t46538852_p25101594131&MSAV=1&msT=1&gss=an gsg&gsfn=James+McKinley&gsln=Sanders&msbdy=1902&msbpn__ftp=Texas &msddy=1978&msdpn__ftp=Fort+Worth%2c+Tarrant%2c+Texas%2c+USA& msrpn__ftp=Texas%2c+USA&msrpn1__ftp=Los+Angeles%2c+Los+Angeles%2 c+California%2c+USA&msrpn2__ftp=Fort+Worth%2c+Tarrant%2c+Texas&ms fng0=James+%27Jimmie%27&msfns0=Sanders&msmng0=Hattie&msmns0=C heney+Sanders+James&cpxt=1&catBucket=rstp&uidh=y53&cp=12&pcat=RO OT_CATEGORY&h=996771&db=txdeathcerts&indiv=1 (July 6, 2014). The October 30, 1903 "In the Courts" section of the *Dallas Morning News* reported that the Tarrant County Clerk's office had recorded the birth of a boy to Mr. and Mrs. James Sanders of Birdville, but this may not be James McKinley Sanders. The Cheney and Sanders family always celebrated James McKinley Sander's birthday on September 4.

17. "Dolly [sic] Cheney, Proof of Heirship," Tarrant County Deed Records, Vol. 1134, 513, Tarrant County Clerk, Fort Worth, Texas; "Inquest is Held over Slain Negro's Body," *Fort Worth Star-Telegram*, March 29, 1915.

18. "Negro is Killed by Cripple," *Fort Worth Star-Telegram*, March 28, 1915, 16.; "Nineteen Indictments Found by Grand Jury," *Fort Worth Star-Telegram*, April 1,1915, 13; "Standard Certificate of Death for Charley James, certificate number 643, March 27, 1915," Death Certificates, Texas State Board of Health, Bureau of Vital Statistics. There is a second death certificate (certificate number 6512) for a "Charlie James" who appears to be the same person and who died under the same circumstances, one day later. March 27 is the correct death date.

19. "Certificate of Death for Major Guerry, certificate number 49853, July 4, 1974," Death Certificates, Texas Department of Health, Bureau of Vital Statistics.

20. "Trying to Tie Himself, He Fell Into Trinity River and Was Drowned," *Fort Worth Morning Register*, September 6, 1900, 4.

21. "2 Negroes Killed Same Spot, 15 Minutes Apart," *Fort Worth Star-Telegram*, September 20, 1914, 6.

22. "Standard Certificate of Death for Lit Borders, certificate number 19351, September 19, 1914," Death Certificates, Texas State Board of Health, Bureau of Vital Statistics.

23. "2 Negroes"; "Negro Charged with Killing Denied Bond," *Fort Worth Star-Telegram*, September 22, 1914, 11.

24. "Chaney [sic] Murder Jury Discharged," *Fort Worth Star-Telegram*, October 17, 1914, 7.

25. "Bad Reputation of Man He Shot Doesn't Save Him," *Fort Worth Star-Telegram*, December 20, 1914, 13.

26. "Polk Chaney [sic] Jailed on Three Charges," *Fort Worth Star-Telegram*, February 11, 1916, 7.

27. "22 Negroes are Selected by Two City Draft Boards," *Fort Worth Star-Telegram*, October 28, 1917, Sect. 2, 6. None of Polk Cheney's service records have survived, but the only photograph of Polk shows him wearing an army enlisted man's uniform.

28. "Negro Fined $25 for Attack on Officer," *Fort Worth Star-Telegram*, November 3, 1915, 11.

29. "Officer Breaks his Gun on Negro's Head as Black is Unruly," *Fort Worth Star-Telegram*, October 3, 1916, 6.

30. "Convict Caught," *Fort Worth Star-Telegram*, November 20, 1916, 2.

31. "Negro Shot," *Fort Worth Star-Telegram*, February 10, 1918, 9. Lon Cheney is mistakenly identified as "Lendy Chaney" in the newspaper article, but a subsequent article published on February 12, 1918, which notes that Cheney had died, identifies him by his correct first name, although the last name is still misspelled.

32. "Standard Certificate of Death for Lonnie Chaney [sic]," Texas Department of Health, Bureau of Vital Statistics, certificate number 9456, filed February 11, 1918; "Negro Dies of Wounds," *Fort Worth Star-Telegram*, February 12, 1918, 11. The City-County Hospital, where Lon Cheney was taken, still stands today at 308 East 4th Street. It is used as offices for Bass Hall support personnel.

33. "Standard Certificate of Death for Land Willie Chaney [sic]," Texas Department of Health, Bureau of Vital Statistics, certificate number 8887, filed April 5, 1921.

34. "Dollie Cheney," 1910 US Census, http://interactive.ancestry.com/7884/4455036_00190/124514470?backurl=http%3a%2f%2fsearch.ancestry.com%2fcgibin%2fsse.dll%3frank%3d1%26new%3d1%26tid%3d46538852%26tpid%3d25103800387%26ssrc%3dpt_t46538852_p25103800387%26MSAV%3d1%26msT%3d1%26gss%3dangsd%26gsfn%3dDollie%26gsln

%3dCheney%2b%26msbdy%3d1887%26msbpn__ftp%3dTexas%26msrpn
__ftp%3dBirdville%252c%2bTarrant%252c%2bTexas%252c%2bUSA
%26msfng0%3dMajor%26msfns0%3dCheney%26msmng0%3dMalinda
%26msmns0%3dCheney%26dbOnly%3d_83004006%257c_83004006_x
%252c_83004005%257c_83004005_x%26uidh%3dy53%26msbng0%3dLan
%26msbns0%3dCheney%26msbng1%3dLon%26msbns1%3dCheney
%26msbng2%3dHattie%26msbns2%3dCheney%26msbng3%3dMary
%26msbns3%3dCheney%26msbng4%3dMckenley%26msbns4%3dCeney
%26msbng5%3dPolk%26msbns5%3dCheney%26msbng6%3dHattie
%26msbns6%3dCheney%2bSanders%2bJames%26pcat%3d35%26h
%3d124514470%26db%3d1910USCenIndex%26indiv%3d1&ssrc=pt
_t46538852_p25103800387&backlabel=ReturnRecord (September 5, 2013).

35. "In the Courts," *Fort Worth Star-Telegram*, May 15, 1916, 7.

36. "Raymond Dennis," *U.S.*, *World War I Draft Registration Cards, 1917-1918*, http://interactive.ancestry.com/6482/005152958_04009/15668625?backurl=http %3a%2f%2fsearch.ancestry.com%2fcgibin%2fsse.dll%3findiv%3dtry%26db%3d WW1draft%26h%3d15668625&ssrc=&backlabel=ReturnRecord (July 6, 2014).

37. "Dolly [sic] Cheney, Proof of Heirship."

38. "Molindy [sic] Cheney, Proof of Heirship," Tarrant County Deed Records, Vol. 882, 387, Tarrant County Clerk, Fort Worth, Texas.

Chapter 8: Sand and Gravel

1. Nancy Beck Young, "Chicago, Rock Island and Gulf Railway," *Handbook of Texas Online*, http://www.tshaonline.org/handbook/online/articles/eqc08, uploaded on June 12, 2010, published by the Texas State Historical Association (July 16, 2014).

2. Tarrant County Commissioners Court Minutes, Vol. 22, 330-332, November 18, 1911.

3. Tarrant County Deed Records, Vol. 351, 353, filed January 3, 1912.

4. Kirk Kite, "Highway Development," *Handbook of Texas Online*, http://www.tshaonline.org/handbook/online/articles/erh02, uploaded on June 15, 2010, published by the Texas State Historical Association (July 16, 2014).

5. W.H. Hawker, et al. *Soil Survey of Tarrant County, Texas* (Washington, DC: Government Printing Office, 1924), 892; Thomas E. Popplewell, *Mining Methods And Costs At the Hart Spur Pit of the Fort Worth Sand & Gravel Co., Inc., Fort Worth, Tex.*(Washington, D.C.: U.S. Dept. of Commerce, Bureau of Mines, 1932), 2.

6. "Fort Worth Sand & Gravel Company Inc." Business Organizations Inquiry, Texas Secretary of State, https://direct.sos.state.tx.us (August 21, 2014); "Ex-Exec Dies at 78," *Fort Worth Star-Telegram*, December 15, 1966, 4.
7. Ibid.
8. Tarrant County Deed Records. Vol. 668, 273, filed April 28, 1921.
9. Tarrant County Deed Records. Vol. 685, 151-152, filed April 18, 1921.
10. Ibid.
11. "Texas Industries to Buy Five Fort Worth Concerns," *Dallas Morning News*, April 3, 1953, 18; "Fortune Changes Hands," *Dallas Morning News*, May 28, 1953, 12.
12. "Golden Date to be Noted by James M. Sanderses," *Fort Worth Star-Telegram*, August 27, 1973, 5F.
13. Tarrant County Deed Records, v. 759, 276, filed January 16, 1923.
14. Ibid.
15. Tarrant County Deed Records, v. 759, 277, filed January 16, 1923.
16. Popplewell, 11.
17. Ibid., 6.
18. Ibid., 10.
19. Tarrant County Deed Records, v. 882, 380, filed August 4, 1925.

Chapter 9: Unraveling: A New Generation and Depressing Times

1. "Standard Certificate of Death for Magor [sic] Cheney," Texas Department of Health, Bureau of Vital Statistics, certificate number 8103, filed February 27, 1925.
2. "Standard Certificate of Death for Polk Cheney," Texas Department of Health, Bureau of Vital Statistics, certificate number 33139, filed September 18, 1926.
3. J.H. Shepherd, Department of Veterans Affairs to Andrew J. Sanders, TLS, February 14, 1992, gives Laura Cheney's death date as July 17, 1978. A listing for a Laura Cheney in the US Social Security Death Index, 1935-2014, indicates that she died in San Jose, California. The listing has the correct date of death and appears to be for Polk's widow, but could possibly be for another individual with the same name and death date (October 30, 2014).
4. "Standard Certificate of Death for Malinda Chaney [sic]," Texas Department of Health, Bureau of Vital Statistics, certificate number 25800, filed May 19, 1931.
5. Hattie and Lillie Hooper to Drew Sanders, personal communication, October 21, 1980.
6. "Cards of Thanks," *Fort Worth Star-Telegram*, May 23, 1931, 20.
7. Tarrant County Deed Records, v. 575, 349.
8. Tarrant County Deed Records. v. 1375, 619.

9.   "Tarrant County to James Sanders," Special Warranty Deed, Tarrant County Deed Records, Vol. 575, 348, filed April 27, 1938; Bob Ray Sanders, "Honoring Pioneer Family's Impact on Area Education," *Fort Worth Star-Telegram*, August 16, 2009, 15A.

10. See, for example, Annie Mae Hollingsworth and Her Brother on a Burro in Front of Their Home, Photograph, n.d.; digital image, (http://texashistory .unt.edu/ark:/67531/metapth19856/ (September 16, 2014), University of North Texas Libraries, The Portal to Texas History, http://texashistory.unt.edu; crediting Tarrant County College NE, Heritage Room, Fort Worth, Texas; Hollingsworth Farmhouse, Photograph, n.d.; digital image, (http://texashistory.unt.edu/ark:/67531/metapth28258/ (September 16, 2014), University of North Texas Libraries, The Portal to Texas History, http://texashis-tory.unt.edu; crediting Tarrant County College NE, Heritage Room, Fort Worth, Texas; "Jumbo Enrolls Singing Cowboy, *Fort Worth Star-Telegram*, August 23, 1936, 2.

11. "Map of Garden of Eden," Tarrant County Plat Records, Vol. 388a, 101; Tarrant County Deed Records, Vol. 1319, 275, filed March 12, 1937.

12. "Birdville, First County Seat, Joins Haltom City." *Fort Worth Star-Telegram*, July 7, 1949, 18.

13. "Delilah Williams Guerry," findagrave.com (August 4, 2014); "Major Guerry," United States World War II Army Enlistment Records, 1938-1946, Ancestry.com (August 4, 2014); Fort Worth City Directory (Dallas and Houston: Morrison & Formey Directory Co., 1941), 386.

14. "Certificate of Death for Major Guerry," Texas Department of Health, Bureau of Vital Statistics, certificate number 49853, filed August 15, 1975.

Chapter 10: Use it up, Wear it out, Make it do . . .

1.   "Bourland Gets $5,500 for Additional Help," *Fort Worth Star-Telegram*, February 8, 1944, 2.

2.   "Valley Baptist Church Begins Services," *Birdville Baptist*, March 1951, 2.

3.   Alex Branch, "Rebuilt Church is a Blessing to us All," *Fort Worth Star-Telegram*, November 21, 2009, 4B; Assessors Abstract of Rural Property ("Tax Card"), Tarrant County, Texas, Abstract No. 1513, No. 1D.

4.   Bob Ray Sanders to Drew Sanders, personal communication, November 3, 2014.

5.   "$10,000 Horse is Found Dead, Mutilated with Two Others," *Fort Worth Star-Telegram*, December 13, 1953, evening edition, 1.

6.   "Man, 60, Admits Shooting 2 Horses Near Birdville," *Fort Worth Star-Telegram*,

December 14, 1953, 1.

7. "Certificate of Death for Dollie D. Chaney [sic]," Texas Department of Health, Bureau of Vital Statistics, certificate number 05361, filed January 31,1974.

8. "Ben R. King and wife, Wilma King, to E. F. Abbott," Warranty Deed, Tarrant County Deed Records, Vol. 1972, 169, filed January 23, 1948.

9. See, for example, *Fort Worth Star-Telegram*, May 7, 1948, 23 or *Fort Worth Star-Telegram*, March 30, 1950, 22.

10. "Joe Louis Addition," Tarrant County Plat Records, Vol. 388-G, 159-160.

11. Molly Ivins, "Fort Worth's Joe Louis Addition," *Texas Observer*, December 25, 1970, 3.

12. "John William 'Bill' Estes," *Fort Worth Star-Telegram*, September 30, 2003, 6B.

13. "J. C. Estes to J. W. Estes," Warranty Deed, Tarrant County Deed Records, Vol. 3940, 441.

14. "Operation biggest in Area," *Fort Worth Star-Telegram*, November 12, 1967, 1.

15. Carl Freund, "Tarrant Sanitarian Handed Suspension," *Dallas Morning News*, August 9, 1969, 5. In 1965, Tarrant County and Estes Service Company joined forces to operate the sanitary landfill. There were many issues, particularly with the operation of an incinerator and the fact that county employees and equipment were used to help run the landfill.

16. Bob Ray Sanders to Carol Roark, personal communication, September 15, 2014.

17. Ivins, 3.

18. "Joe Louis Residents on Council Agenda," *Fort Worth Star-Telegram*, November 20, 1970, 4A.

19. Ivins, 4.

20. Ibid., 3.

21. Ibid.

22. Mike Buchholz, "Woman's Home Razed in Confusion-Laden Incident," *Fort Worth Star-Telegram*, 4A.

Chapter 11: A New Generation of Sanderses

1. The Riverside Colored School opened in 1906 in space leased from Corinth Baptist Church. A wood-frame building constructed in 1907 was replaced by a two-room brick school building in 1911. That building still stands today at 2629 N. LaSalle Street. It was used as a school until 1950. See "Riverside Colored Public School" entry in *Tarrant County Historic Resources Survey: Fort Worth: Upper North, Northeast, East, Far South, and Far West* (Fort Worth: Historic Preservation Council), 67.

2. "Fort Worth Housing Authority Administration Building," http://www.fortworthar-

chitecture.com/east/fwha.htm (September 26, 2014).

3. Bennie Ruth Dickens to Drew Sanders, personal communication, September 30, 2014. Seat belts were not required in automobiles until 1968.

4. Opal Trigg used a different word in referring to Buddy, but the author made a decision not to print that term in light of its offensive nature.

5. Bob Ray Sanders, "Mama 'Nez had the Recipe for Life," *Fort Worth Star-Telegram*, June 2, 2002, Metro, 1.

6. "Chamberlin L. Sanders," U. S. World War II Navy Muster Rolls, 1938-1949; "USS *General W. A. Mann*," Wikipedia, http://en.wikipedia.org/wiki/USS _General_W._A._Mann_(AP-112) (September 25, 2014).

7. The Universal Mills/Allied Mills facility still stands at 455 North Beach Street. See page 72 in the *Tarrant County Historic Resources Survey: Fort Worth Upper North, Northeast, East, Far South, and Far West* (Fort Worth: Historic Preservation Council, 1989) for additional information.

8. "Healthcare Heroes," Fort Worth Business Press, January 24, 2003, 10; Chris Vaughn, "Living Legends Awards Will Honor Five in Fort Worth," *Fort Worth Star-Telegram*, June 18, 2008, 3B.

Chapter 12: Rebuilding Community
in the Twenty-first Century

1. Dan X. McGraw, "Love Thy Neighborhood," *Fort Worth Star-Telegram*, June 3, 2006, 1B; Brenda Sanders-Wise to Drew Sanders, personal communication, September 30, 2014.

2. *Guidelines for the Garden of Eden Carson Street Historic District*, Fort Worth Planning and Development Department, City of Fort Worth, Texas, http://fortworth-texas.gov/uploadedFiles/Planning/Historic_Preservation/Guidelines%20for%20the %20Garden%20of%20Eden%20Historic%20District(4).pdf (September 30, 2014), 1.

3. Ibid, 2.

4. Kimberly Wilson, "Fort Worth Man, 60, Fatally Shot," Fort Worth Star-Telegram, August 4, 1996, 22; Stephen G. Michaud and Bob Ray Sanders, "Dragoo Gets Life in Murder of Black Man—Killer Still Insists Race Wasn't Motive," *Fort Worth-Star Telegram*, April 22, 1997, Metro1.

5. Bob Ray Sanders, "Answered Prayers let her Return Home," *Fort Worth Star-Telegram*, April 26, 2006, 1B.

6. John Kirsch, "Black cemetery gets Historical Designation, *Fort Worth Star-Telegram*, October 6, 2006, 1B.

7. McGraw, 1B; Traci Shurley, "Garden of Eden Top Neighborhood," *Fort Worth Star-Telegram*, May 28, 2006, 7B.
8. McGraw, 1B.
9. Bryon Okada, "N. Texas Weathers Storms," *Fort Worth Star-Telegram*, December 30, 2007, 4B.
10. Alex Branch, "Rebuilt Church is a blessing to us all," *Fort Worth Star-Telegram*, November 21, 2009, 4B. The Beck Group specializes in church design and construction and has built church facilities throughout the nation.
11. Bob Ray Sanders, "Honoring Pioneer Family's Impact on Area Education," *Fort Worth Star-Telegram*, August 16, 2009, 15A.

BIBLIOGRAPHY

Books

Boethel, Paul. *History of Lavaca County*, Rev. Ed. Austin: Von Boeckmann-Jones, 1959.

Boyd, Gregory A., ed., *Texas Land Survey Maps for Tarrant County, With Roads, Railways, Waterways, Towns, Cemeteries & Cross-referenced Indexes from the Texas Railroad Commission and General Land Office*. Norman, OK: Arphax Publishing Co., 2008.

Eddins, Eyvonne Andrews, Betty Porter, and David Vorhees, *Birdville, Texas: Frontier Wilderness, County Seat, & Beyond*. Haltom City, TX: Birdville Historical Society, 2005.

Garrett, Julia Kathryn, *Fort Worth: A Frontier Triumph*. Austin: Encino Press, 1972. Reprinted with a foreword by Jenkins Garrett and an index. Fort Worth: TCU Press, 1996.

Howell, Kenneth W., ed., *Still the Arena of Civil War: Violence and Turmoil in Reconstruction Texas*. Denton: University of North Texas Press, 2012.

Smith, David Paul. *Frontier Defense in the Civil War: Texas' Rangers and Rebels*. College Station: Texas A&M University Press, 1992.

Tarrant County Historic Resources Survey Fort Worth: Central Business District. Fort Worth: Historic Preservation Council, 1991.

Tarrant County Historic Resources Survey Fort Worth: Upper North, Northeast, East, Far South, and Far West. Fort Worth: Historic Preservation Council, 1989.

Manuscripts and Photographs

Barry Crouch Collection, Victoria College

Officers and Force of First National Bank, Fort Worth, University of Texas at San Antonio. Photograph Collection, Accession number 81-0726.

Drew Sanders Collection

Billy W. Sills Center for Archives, Fort Worth Independent School District.

Interviews

Mittie Coleman, interview by author, March 24, 1976.

Bennie Ruth Dickens, interview by author, September 30, 2014.

Nun Fretwell, interview by author, July 16, 1981.

Hattie and Lillie Hooper, interview by author, October 21, 1980.

Bibliography

Doug Kubicek, interview by Carol Roark, June 14, 2013.

Bob Ray Sanders, interview by Carol Roark, September 15, 2014.

Brenda Sanders-Wise, interview by author, September 30, 2014.

Newspapers and Periodicals

Dallas Morning News

Fort Worth Business Press

Fort Worth City Directory

Fort Worth Daily Democrat

Fort Worth Daily Gazette

Fort Worth Morning Register

Fort Worth Star-Telegram

Fort Worth Telegram

Texas State Gazette (Austin)

Bruce Glasrud, "Jim Crow's Emergence in Texas," *American Studies*. 15 (1974).

Molly Ivins, "Fort Worth's Joe Louis Addition," *Texas Observer*, December 25, 1970.

Smith, Helena Huntington, "Sam Bass and the Myth Machine," *The American West*. January 1970: 31-35.

Tucson City Directory

Public Records

Clerk Returns, Colorado County, Texas.

Colorado County Deed Records

Colorado County Tax Rolls

Guidelines for the Garden of Eden Carson Street Historic District. Fort Worth Planning and Development Department. City of Fort Worth, Texas. http://fortworthtexas .gov/uploadedFiles/Planning/Historic_Preservation/Guidelines%20for%20the %20Garden%20of%20Eden%20Historic%20District(4).pdf.

Hawker, W. H., et al. *Soil Survey of Tarrant County*, Texas. Washington, DC: Government Printing Office, 1924.

Lavaca County Deed Records

Lavaca County Tax Rolls

Popplewell, Thomas E. *Mining Methods And Costs At the Hart Spur Pit of the Fort Worth Sand & Gravel Co., Inc., Fort Worth, Tex.* Washington, D.C.: U.S. Dept. of Commerce, Bureau of Mines, 1932.

Robertson Preemption Grants, Texas General Land Office.

J.H. Shepherd, Department of Veterans Affairs to Andrew J. Sanders, TLS, February 14, 1992.

Tarrant County Commissioner Court Minutes

Tarrant County Court Minute Books

Tarrant County Deed Records

Tarrant County Plat Records

Tarrant County Tax Rolls

Tarrant County Marriage Records

Texas Death Certificates

Texas Muster Roll Index Cards, 1838-1900.

Business Organizations Inquiry, Texas Secretary of State (https://direct.sos.state.tx.us).

United States Census

United States World War I Draft Registration Cards

United States World War II Army Enlistment Records, 1938-1946.

Websites

www.ancestry.com

www.birdvillehistory.org

www.chickasawcountyhistorical.com

www.familysearch.org

www.findagrave.com

www.fold3.com

Handbook of Texas Online

Portal to Texas History, http://texashistory.unt.edu

www.thecorinthfamily.org

http://en.wikipedia.org/wiki/USS_General_W._A._Mann_(AP-112)

Sanborn Fire Insurance Maps

INDEX

Page numbers in Roman type reference text; italics reference images.

Abbott and Newman Sand and Gravel Company, 121

Abbott, Eulice Foy "Slick," 119, 121-22, 124-25

Adame, Arthur "Chano," 164

Adams, Mr. and Mrs. Cato and family, 126

agriculture, 6-7, 13, 15, 20-21, 23, 25, 28-29, 31, 36, 43-46, 49-51, 60, 70-71, 107-10, 130; *112*

Akers, George, 25

alcoholism, 100-101

Allen, Mrs. Mary and family, 126

Amon Carter-Riverside High School, 15, 64

Anderson, W. C., 73

Anglin, Jerry, 144

Arizona, 79, 85, 97, 123

Armour and Company, 75

Baker Brothers Company, 102

Baker, Edward L., 102

Baker, James B., 102

Baldwin, Mr. and Mrs., 126

Barkley, Benjamin Franklin, 25-26, 28, 74; *26*

Barkley, Francina Alice, 27-28; *27*

Barkley, Leonidas "Lon," 27-28, 74; *27*

Barkley, Malinda, 25, 28-29, 74

Barton, Ida May, 78, 80, 166

Bass, Sam, 35-39

Battercake Flats, 80

Bear Creek, 4, 134-135

Beck Group, 157

Beckham, Robert E., 33-34

Bell, Amie, 67

Bell, Johnnie B., 63-64, 169

Bell, Lindsay, 78

Bell, Rev. John, 67

Big Fossil Creek, 29

Billings, R. R., 125-26

Birdville, ix-x, 1, 6, 8-9, 23, 24, 25, 27-28, 31, 35-38, 42, 61, 69, 72-73, 97, 99, 104, 140, 158; *8-9, 24, 72, 97*

Birdville Baptist Church, 110

Birdville Cemetery, 28

Birdville Colored School, 73, 128, 158

Birdville (Haltom) High School, x, 148

Birdville Independent School District, x, 25, 73, 128, 145, 148, 158-59

Birdville Road, 69, 86

Birdville Union, 23

Blaylock, Mr. and Mrs. A. J. "Biggum" and family, 126

Blaylock, Mr. and Mrs. Jack and family, 126

Bloodgood, C. M., 32, 179

Boaz, Agnes, 23, 171

Boaz, Aurelia Jane Hampton, 29, 94, 167

Boaz, Clara. *See* Wilson, Clara

Boaz, Clysta, 29, 167

Boaz, Copeland, 29, 168

Boaz, Cunard, 29, 168

Boaz, David, 171

Boaz, Ed, 29, 73, 94, 167

Boaz, Elizabeth Sarah, 171

Boaz, George W., 29, 167

Boaz, Hezekiah, 171

Boaz, Mary, 29, 168

Boaz, Mary Frances, 171
Boaz, Rachel, 29
Boaz, Richard, 171
Boaz, Robert Leonidas, 171
Boaz, Samuel, 2, 23, 29, 171
Boaz, Sarah. *See* Johnson, Sarah
Boaz, William Jesse "W. J.," 171
Bob Jones Park/Bob Jones Nature Center,
    70
Boethel, Paul C., 19
Bonner, H. P., 88
Boone, Manerva and John, 36
Booth, Judge, 67
Booth, Landon, 41
Borders, Lit, 78
Bowman, [Martha E.], 32-33, 179
Brashears, Damie, 73
Brazer, George, 67
Brockman, Frank, 61
Brooks, Reverend, 67
Brown, Dorothy "Peaches." *See* Sanders,
    Dorothy Brown
Brown, Mr. and Mrs. Jeff and family, 126
Brown, Mr. and Mrs. Joe and family, 126
Brown, Mrs. Nadine and family, 126
Brown, Quincy, 145
Brown, Reverend, 113
Buffalo Soldiers, 12
Bureau of Refugees, Freedmen, and Aban-
    doned Lands, 21, 26, 28
Burnett, Ann Valliant. *See* Tandy, Ann Val-
    liant Burnett
Burnett, Anne Valliant, 171
Burnett, Frances, 171
Burnett, Frank M., 171
Burnett, Olive "Ollie" Lake, 171
Burnett, Ruth B. Loyd, 171
Burnett, Samuel Burk, 171
Burnett, Thomas Loyd, 171

Burse, Don, 155
Bussey Farm, *112*
Bussey, Anita and Tom, 148
Bussey, Julius, 148
Butler, Joe, 144

Calton, Mrs. and family, 126
Camp Colorado, 12
Camp Cooper, 12
Camp Salmon, 10, 12
Capps, Isham, 34
Carey, Mrs. C. B., 123, 126
Carey, Mrs. Preston and family, 126
Carson Street, 1, 8, 42, 73, 94-95, 102,
    105, 149, 158
Carson Street Garden of Eden Historic
    and Cultural Landmark District, 154
Carter, Bruce, 155
Caruthers, Mr. and Mrs. and family, 126
Carver, George Washington Elementary/
    Junior High School, 129-30
Carver Heights, 154
Cattle, xi, 9-10, 15, 19-20, 28, 31, 41-44,
    64-65, 70, 134, 137
Cauthern, Curtis, 144
Central Wagon Yard, 31
Champagne, Clara, 73
Chapman, James W., 73
Cheney, A. Jane, 170
Cheney, Alzada, 40, 170
Cheney, Aquilla, 170
Cheney, Arthur K. Polk, 170
Cheney, Catherine, 40, 170
Cheney, Catherine Evans Owen, 16, 170
Cheney, Charlotte Shaw, 17, 170
Cheney, Dollie, 35, 38-39, 41, 44-45, 73-
    74, 82-85, 94, 96-101, 104-05, 110,
    116-19, 117, 121, 130, 137, 140, 143,
    149, 151-52, 157, 166; 82, *117*

Cheney, Elizabeth "Eliza" J. Watts, 3, 20, 35, 40-41, 170
Cheney, Francis Marion, 16, 169
Cheney, Hattie. *See* Sanders, Hattie Cheney
Cheney, Dr. Jasper Newton, 170
Cheney, John G., 16-17, 20-21, 35-36, 39-41, 169
Cheney, John O., 40-41, 169
Cheney, John Richard "Dick," Jr., 16-21, 169
Cheney, John, Sr., 16, 169
Cheney, Joseph, 170
Cheney, Landen "Lan" or "Land Willie," 74, 78, 83, 166
Cheney, Laura Gilbert, 79, 85, 97, 166, 186
Cheney, Leonidas "Lon," 41, 74, 78-80, 83, 166
Cheney, Lewis Rabon, 16-17, 19, 169
Cheney, Lucy Evans Owen, 16-17, 20, 169
Cheney, Major, x, 3, 15, 18-20, 22, 35-50, 62-67, 69, 72-76, 78, 80, 83-84, 86, 89, 91, 94, 96, 98-102, 105, 128-29, 149-52, 156, 158-59, 162, 166, 170, 176; *43*
Cheney, Malinda Loyd, 2, 4, 7, 13, 15, 29, 35, 39-41, 43, 46-51, 57-58, 62-63, 66-67, 69, 72-74, 76-78, 83-84, 89, 91, 94, 96-100, 102, 105, 110, 121, 128, 149-52, 156, 158, 162, 166; *77*
Cheney, Mary. *See* Guerry, Mary Cheney
Cheney, Mary A. Preston, 170
Cheney, Mary Owen, 16, 169
Cheney, McKinley, 74-75, 78, 166
Cheney, Polk, 74, 78-79, 84-85, 94, 96-97, 166; *81*
Cheney, Rachel Benson, 16, 169

Cheney, Samuel, 170
Cheney Settlement, 19-20
Cheney, Trina, 41
Cheney, William D., 170
Chicago, Rock Island and Gulf Railway (Rock Island), 29, 86, 89, 92
Chicago, Rock Island and Texas Railway, 32
Chicken and Dumplings, Old Fashioned, 51-52
Chitlin's and Hog Maws, 53-54
Chumley, Roy, 157
City Carriage and Wagon Shop, 31-32
City-County Hospital, 135, 184
Civil War, 2-3, 5, 13, 21, 23, 25, 28
Clayton, William, 169
Coleman, William, 73
Colorado and Southern Railroad, 64
Colorado County, 17, 20
Confederates, 10, 13, 21, 28, 34
cookbook, 155-56
Copeland, Carolina, 67
Corinth Baptist Church, 66-67, 69, 75-76, 78, 94, 96, 99, 110, 188; *66*
Cornbread, Mama 'Nez's Hot Water, 56
cotton, 7, 20-21, 23, 51, 60
Covington, Mr. and Mrs. Henry and family, 126
Cowan, Sarah and Alonzo, 61
Cowanville, 61
Crane, Mr. and Mrs. Ruben and family, 126

Daggett, E. M. "Bud," 70
Daggett, Ruby, 79
Dallas/Fort Worth International Airport, 60-61
Daniels, Joe, 144
Davis, Amanda Robins, 61-63, 168; *62*

Davis, Annie, 63, 169
Davis, Bennie Daggett, 63, 169
Davis, Jim, 67
Davis, Julius, 63, 168
Davis, Katie Bell, 63, 169
Davis, Mack, 61, 63, 168
Davis, Mack, Jr., 63, 169
Davis, Mollie, 63, 169
Davis, Rosa, 67
Davis, Warren, 63, 169
Davis, Winnie, 63, 169
Dennard, J. Daniel, Jr., 80
Dennis, Dollie Cheney. *See* Cheney, Dollie
Dennis, Raymond, 85, 166
Denton, Texas, 36, 38
domestic chores, 43, 46, 48-49, 51, 104, 108, 130, 137-38, 152
Dove, 4, 59, 68, 70
Duckett, Mr. and Mrs. Ollie and family, 126
Duckett, Mr. and Mrs. Samuel and family, 126

Ebenezer Baptist Church, 61
education, 72-73
Elder, Mr. and Mrs. and family, 126
Elliott Reeder Road, 29, 42, 94, 110-111, 118, 122, 157-58
Ellis Pecan Co., xi
Egypt, 4
Estes, J. C., 123
Estes, John William "Bill," 122-23
Estes Service Company (Estes Dump), 123-25, 124, 194; *124*
Evans, Mr. and Mrs. Marshall and family, 126

Farmer, Marshal Sam, 34

Federal Aid Road Act, 87
Felder, Senola. *See* Howard, Senola Felder
Fellowship Church—Grapevine, 157
Fenley, Tennessee, 67
Fennell, Odis, 73
First National Bank, 13-14
Foley, Washington Green Lee, 17
Ford, Mr. and Mrs. Herman and family, 127
Ford, Mr. and Mrs. Nash and family, 127
Ford, Mr. and Mrs. Oscar and family, 127
Fort Worth, ix-x, 1, 5, 25, 28, 31-32, 46, 61, 63, 67, 78-80, 83, 86, 88, 93, 102, 113, 122, 125-26, 129, 135, 136-38, 145, 151, 154
Fort Worth Comets, 145
Fort Worth Concrete Company, 121
Fort Worth Convention Center, 32
Fort Worth Historic and Cultural Landmarks Commission, 154
Fort Worth Independent School District, 67, 145
Fort Worth Sand and Gravel, 84, 88-97, 91, 93, 99-101, 108, 110, 115-16, 121, 125-26 134, 137, 145, 149; 90, 91, 93
Fort Worth Star-Telegram, 57, 79-80, 85, 98-99, 113, 122, 145-46, 152
Fort Worth Warriors, 145
Fort Worth Zoo, xi
Fried Chicken, 54-55
Free people of color (before Civil War), 1-2, 19-20
Freedmen (after Civil War), 4, 21-22, 26-27, 60, 70, 134
Freedmen's Bureau. *See* Bureau of Refugees, Freedmen, and Abandoned Lands
French, Mr. and Mrs. Gomillion and family, 127
Fretwell, Carl, 96

Fretwell Cemetery, 69
Fretwell, Nun Q., 73, 75, 96-97, 99
Fretwell, Rev. Greene, 69, 96
Frontier Regiment, 10, 12-13

garbage dump/landfill, 108, 122-26
Garcia, Alicia. *See* Sanders, Alicia "Lisa"
Garden of Eden Neighborhood Association, 153, 155, 159
Gentry, Dollie Sanders, 142-44, 152, 165; *115, 142*
Gentry, Henry L., Jr., 143, 165; 115
Gentry, Henry L., III, 165
Gentry, Niphateria "Nip," 165
Gentry, Pamela "Pam," 165
George, Clyde, 144
George, Raymond, 144
Georgia's Café, 104
Giddens, Kelly, 157
Gilbert, Laura. *See* Cheney, Laura Gilbert
Gilstrap, Mr. and Mrs. Willie and family, 127
good roads movement, 86-88
Grapevine Auctioneers, 140, 145
Grapevine, Texas, 1, 59, 71, 140, 145, 157
Great Depression, 99-100, 150
Guerry, Delilah "Lila" Mae Williams, 102, 166
Guerry, John, 66, 76, 166
Guerry, Lottie and Burton, family, 66-67
Guerry, Major, 3, 76 78, 80, 83-84, 94, 96-97, 99-102, 151, 166; *77*
Guerry, Mary Cheney 41, 66, 74, 76, 78, 166

Hall, James Goodwin, 171
Hall, Otis and Martha, 127
Hallettsville, 18, 21
Haltom City, Texas, ix, 25, 102, 121-23, 125, 129, 156-58
Haltom High School, x, 148
Hardgraves, Gerald, 144
Harris Hospital School of Nursing, 143
Hart, J. O., 88
Hart Spur, 89-90, 92
Heistead, W. H., 21
Henderson, Sheriff Joe, 33-34
Henry P. Tuggle Survey, 91
High, Bo, 127
High, Shirley, 127
Hill, the, 71
Hodge Station, 42, 59, 64, 66, 67, 86; *65*
Hogan, Cessely. *See* Sanders, Cessely Hogan
Hogs, 44, 53-54, 107-08, 110; *106*
Hooper, Gid, 67, 73
Hooper, Hattie, 41, 75-76, 99
Hooper, Lillie, 41, 75-76, 99
Hot Water Cornbread, Mama 'Nez's, 56
Howard, Frank, 63, 168
Howard, Jess, 168
Howard, Jessie, 63, 168
Howard, Senola Felder, 63, 168
Hudson, Charles, 144
Hughes, Rev. C. P., 67
Hunter, Junior, 144

incinerator, 123-25, 188; *124*
Indian Removal Act, 16-17
Indians. *See* Native Americans
Ivins, Molly, 125

Jack and the Jivers, 144-45
Jackson, Columbus, 79
Jackson, Reverend and family, 127
Jackson, Will, 83
James, Charley, 76, 166
Jefferson, Bernice Sanders, 105, 127, 140-

42, 164; *115*

Jefferson, Floretta Diana "Dinky," 164

Jefferson, Floyd, 127, 141, 164; *115*

Jefferson, Kareem "Slugger," 164

Jefferson, Millie, 164

Jefferson, Paranell, 164

Jefferson, Phillippa "Leapy," 164

Jefferson, Ron, 164

Jefferson, Tammulia "Tammy," 164

Jefferson, Tarvis, 164

Jim Crow. *See* segregation

Joe Louis Addition, 119-27, 120-23, 141, 153, 155; *120, 121, 123*

John Akers Survey, 36, 91

John B. York Survey, 15

John Walker Survey, 36

Johns, Marilla and Nathaniel, 70

Johnson, Bennie Ruth, 105

Johnson, Charles A., 171

Johnson, Dilsie and Robert, 58, 60

Johnson, Edith. *See* Sanders, Edith

Johnson, Herbert, 113

Johnson, Herbert, Jr., 155

Johnson, Jimmy, 29, 94, 168

Johnson, Josephine, 155

Johnson, Lucinda. *See* Sadler, Lucinda

Johnson, Sarah Boaz, 29, 94, 168

Jones, Almeada, 70

Jones, Jinks, 70

Jones, John Dolford "Bob," 70; *68*

Jones, John Emory, 70

Jones, Leazer, 70

Jones, Mr. and Mrs. Homer and family, 127

Jones, Mr. and Mrs. Y. D. and family, 127

Jordan, Bill, 71

Juneteenth, 3, 70

Keith, Dessic, 78, 166

Kentucky, 5-7, 23, 25

KERA, 146

King, Ben R., 119

King James and the Galaxies, 144

King James and the Rocking Teens, 144

Kingsbury, Dr. H. B., 96, 101

Kingsbury, Robert, 121

Ku Klux Klan, 28

Kubicek, Doug, 17

Lake Grapevine, 70

Lake, Mary Daggett, 70

Land grants, 17-18, 31, 150

Lavaca County, 17-21, 35-36

Lee, Lucy, 60

Lewis, Joseph, 31

Lewis, Robert, 31

LifeGift, 143

Littlejohn, Calvin, 148

Little Fossil Creek, 28-29, 102

Lott, Tommy, 144

Louder, Elie, 67

Louis, Joe, 122

Loyd, Abe, 29, 166

Loyd, Charlotte, 6-7, 9, 13, 15, 23, 29, 39, 67, 78, 166

Loyd, Dick, 29, 167

Loyd, Eliza "Liza," 10, 29, 167

Loyd, Emma, 13, 29, 166

Loyd, Green, 5-7, 9, 12-15, 23, 29, 31, 39, 41, 64, 67, 69, 73, 78, 150-51, 166; *14*

Loyd, Hale C., 5-8, 11, 13, 15, 29, 31, 170

Loyd, Hannah "Annie" Reed, 167

Loyd, Harold W., 167

Loyd, Henry, 7, 29, 166

Loyd, Ida. *See* McClardy, Ida Loyd

Loyd, Julia, 10, 29, 167

Loyd, Laura Buckner, 167

Loyd, Lee, 166

Loyd, Malinda. *See* Malinda Loyd Cheney
Loyd, Margaret A. M. Valliant, 170
Loyd, Martin, 29, 166
Loyd, Martin Bottom "M. B.," 6, 8-15, 14, 33, 29, 170; *11*, *14*
Loyd, Mary Ann. *See* McClardy, Mary Ann "Lollie" Loyd
Loyd, Missouri Stoval, 166
Loyd, Oscar, 73, 167
Loyd, Rebecca W. Bottoms, 5-6, 11, 29, 170
Loyd, Rush, 7, 31-34, 41-42, 73, 78, 119, 150-51, 167
Loyd, Rush, Jr., 167
Loyd, Sadie, 119, 121, 167
Loyd, Sarah, 166
Loyd, Thomas P., 6, 11, 15, 170
Lower Birdville, 36
lynching, attempted, 32-34

Major Cheney Elementary School at South Birdville, 158-59; *159*
Maryland, 16
Mason, Curtis, 163
Massay, Dallas, 13; *14*
Mathes, Bill, 67
Matthews, Susan, 67
Mayes, Leslie, 6, 171; *14*
Mayfield Baptist Church, 61
McCarver, Mr. and Mrs. Ray and family, 127
McClardy, George, Jr., 167; *64*
McClardy, George, Sr., 167; *64*
McClardy, Ida Loyd, 29, 67, 167; *64*
McClardy, Manda, 167; *64*
McClardy, Mary Ann "Lollie" Loyd, 29, 167
McClardy, Minnie, 167; *64*

McClardy, Nicholas, 167; *64*
McClardy, Samantha, 167; *64*
McClardy, Spencer, 167; *64*
McClardy, Wesley, 167
McCord, James E., 10, 12
McDonald, Mr. and Mrs. Eddie and family, 127
McDonald, Walter Earl, 144
McDonald, Willie Esther, 127
McEwen, Maggie, 73
McKee, Lillie, 67
Meat Loaf, Mama 'Nez's, 52-53
Miller, Mrs. Catherine and family, 127
Mississippi, 6-7, 31, 36
Mississippi River, 7, 36, 84,
Morris, John, 34
Mosier Valley, 4, 50, 59-61, 140; *59*, *60*
Moss, Frank, 155
Mount Carmel Baptist Church, 70
Mount Gilead Baptist Church, 67
Mount Horuhm Baptist Church, 71
Mrs. Baird's Bread, 85
mulatto, 19
murder, 21, 78-79, 83, 155

Native Americans, 2, 6, 12, 16-17, 39, 61
Navidad Nation, 19-22
Navidad River, 17-19
Neighborhoods USA—Neighborhood of the Year, 155
New Trinity Cemetery, 69, 75, 96-97, 99, 155
Nichols, Oscar, 169
North Dallas, 4
North Side Colored School, 128-30; *129*
North Texas Negro League, 140

1-2-3-4 (one-two-three-four) cakes, 57
Owen, Catherine Evans, 16, 170

Owen, Lucy Evans, 16-17, 20, 169

Palo Pinto County, 7, 9-10, 13
Pecan Pound Cake, Malinda Cheney's, 37
pecans, xi, 28, 41, 44-45, 57
Pelham, 4
Pendleton, William S., 33
Pennerson, Dicky, 144
People's Burial Park, 69
Phillips, Ms. Billie and family, 127
Phillips, Ms. Ellen and family, 127
poll tax, 5
pollution, 75, 124-25
Polytechnic, 61
post office, 27-28, 138, 151
Prairie View A & M College, 140
Prairie View Interscholastic League, 132, 134

Quakertown, 4
Quigley, R. M., 88-89

Ransom, Dr. Riley, Sr., 136-37; *136*
recipes, 51-58
Recipes from Out to the House: Seasoned with Soul, 155-56
Reconstruction, 5, 28, 40
Reed, Lucy and George, 31
Rice, Rev. Isaiah and Margaret, 127
Ritz Theatre, 137-38
Riverside, 29, 41, 59, 64, 66-67, 69, 73, 75-76, 78, 102, 118, 140
Riverside Colored School, 67, 69, 73, 76, 94, 129-30, 188-89
Riverside Elementary School, viii, x, 129; *129*
Riverside Independent School District, 67
Republic of Texas, 2, 17
robbery, 36-39

Roberson, Lilly. *See* Sanders, Lilly Rose Roberson
Robertson's Colony, 31
Robinson, Chorlette Sanders, 163; *153*
Robinson, Silas, 168
Rolla, Lenora, 92
Ross family, *112*
Runaway Scrape, 17
Rush Loyd Survey, 31
Russell, Dan Moody, Sr., 140, 164; *115*
Russell, Dan "Pooney," Jr., 164
Russell, Lillette Michelle "Shelly," 164
Russell, Patricia "Tweet," 164
Russell, Ruben and Dora and family, 127
Russell, Virgil Lucinda Sanders, 140, 164; *115*

Saddler, Lonnie "Brer," 144
Sadler, Alwyn, 138, 163
Sadler, Alwyn, Jr., 163
Sadler, Hillman, 104-105, 168; *111*
Sadler, Lucinda "Aunt Cindy" Johnson, 29, 104-105, 149, 152, 168; *30, 103*
Samuel Elliott Survey, 32, 119
Sanders, Alicia Garcia "Lisa," 143, 165
Sanders, Andrew James "Buddy," 47, 50, 61, 89, 91, 105, 110, 113, 132-38, 140, 148-49, 152-53, 163; *115, 133, 153*
Sanders, Andrew James "Drew," Jr., ix-xii, 91, 137-138, 148, 163; *xiv, 141, 153*
Sanders, Bernice. *See* Jefferson, Bernice Sanders
Sanders, Beverly Tolliver, 143, 165; *115*
Sanders, Bob Ray, ix-xii, 116, 118, 137-138, 145-146, 148, 152, 165; *viii, 115, 146*
Sanders, Brenda. *See* Sanders-Wise, Brenda

Sanders, Bruce McKinley, 163
Sanders, Cedric, 164
Sanders, Cessely Hogan, 145, 165
Sanders, Chamberlin L. "Chink," 140,
    148, 157, 163; *115, 139*
Sanders, Chamberlin L. "Lucky," Jr., 163
Sanders, Chanalene, 163
Sanders, Chandon, 165
Sanders, Chaney, Sr., 105, 127, 130-31,
    163; *115*
Sanders, Chaney "Scrappy" Jr., 163
Sanders, Chorlette. *See* Robinson, Chor-
    lette Sanders
Sanders, Daniel, 165
Sanders, Debra "Red," 165
Sanders, Delbert, Jr., 165
Sanders, Delbert, Sr., 113-114, 142-43,
    165; *115*
Sanders, Dollie. *See* Gentry, Dollie
    Sanders
Sanders, Dorothy Brown, 146, 148, 165
Sanders, Dr., 63, 168
Sanders, Edith, 164
Sanders, Edith Johnson, ix, 29, 55, 94-95,
    104-05, 110, 115, 118-19, 122, 130-
    31, 133, 135, 137, 140, 142, 144-45,
    148-49, 152, 162, 168, 177-178; *30,
    103, 147*
Sanders, Edward, 113-14, 130, 132, 164;
    115
Sanders, Gerald, 165
Sanders, Gladys Trigg, 61, 140, 148-49,
    163
Sanders, Hattie, 148, 163
Sanders, Hattie Cheney, 41, 62-63, 74-76,
    78, 162, 166, 168
Sanders, Hattie Mae. *See* Sedberry, Hattie
    Mae Sanders
Sanders, Inez Trigg, 61, 105, 134-38, 148-
    49, 152-53, 163; *115, 139, 141, 153*
Sanders, James Edward, 164
Sanders, James "Jimmy," 62-63, 75, 78,
    162, 168
Sanders, James McKinley "Dick Cheney,"
    ix, 75-76, 80, 83-84, 89, 93-97, 99-
    102, 104-5, 107-110, 113-116, 118-
    19, 130, 133, 135, 137, 140, 142,
    144-45, 148-49, 151-52, 162, 168,
    183; *77, 109, 147*
Sanders, James McKinley "Dooney," Jr.,
    113, 144-45, 165; *115*
Sanders, Jaquita "Jaqui," 165
Sanders, Joan Holbert, 127, 131, 163; *115*
Sanders, Johnny Zero, ix, 145, 165
Sanders, Josephine High, 163; *115*
Sanders, LaQueta, 164
Sanders, Leta Jo, 165
Sanders, Lilly Rose Roberson, 131, 163
Sanders, Lucinda. *See* Russell, Virgil Lu-
    cinda Sanders
Sanders, Michael, 165
Sanders, Michaelangelo Antoine, 163; *153*
Sanders, Orlando, 165
Sanders, Paul, 163
Sanders, Phillip R., 163; *153*
Sanders, Precilla, 165
Sanders, Reginald "Reggie," 164
Sanders, Robert Earl, 163
Sanders, Rosa Lee Bettis, 132, 164
Sanders, Rose Marie Byas, 164
Sanders, Sharon, 164
Sanders, Thomas Earl, 163; *141*
Sanders, Thyra, 164
Sanders, Timothy, 163; *153*
Sanders, Trina, 154, 163; *153*
Sanders-Trigg Family Choir, 138, 145, 148
Sanders-Wise, Brenda, 148, 152-54, 163;
    153

school integration, 129, 131, 148, 158

Sedberry, Cecil, 138, 163

Sedberry, Hattie Mae Sanders, 133, 138, 163; *115, 139*

segregation, ix, xi, 40, 73, 128-129, 150-151

Shaw, Mr. and Mrs. Robert "Pa" and family, 127

Shoe Shine Red, 145

Shoemaker, F. E., 171

slavery, x, xii, 1-7, 13-17, 19-21, 23, 25-26, 29, 31, 40, 60, 69-70, 150, 170

Smith, Cassandra, 164

Smith, Imogene and Harry, 127

Smith, Rev. W. C., 75-76

Sneed, Mr. and Mrs. James and family, 127

Sneed, Mr. and Mrs. William and family, 127

Snell, Mr. and Mrs. Ollie and family, 127

South Birdville Elementary School, 158

Southlake, Texas, 70

Stock, Jerome, 157

Stop Six, 4, 59, 61-63, 154

Stovall, Craig, 157

Sunday dinner, 48, 51, 113, 138, 152, 156; *50*

Sweet Potatoes, Mama Edith's Baked, 55

Sylvania Park, xi

Tandy, Anne Valliant Burnett, 171

Tandy, Charles, 171

Tarrant County, ix-x, 1-2, 5-6, 8, 13, 15, 23-26, 28-29, 31-33, 36, 39-42, 59-60, 70-71, 73, 86-87, 108, 122-24, 155-56

Tarrant County Commissioners, 86, 108

Tarrant County Jail, 33-34; *33*

Tarrant County Registration Board, 26

Tea Cakes, Malinda Cheney's, 58

Terrell Heights, 154

Terrell, I. M., High School, 73, 128-30, 132-34, 138, 140-44, 148; *131*

Terrell, Isaiah Milligan, 128-29

Texas, 1-2, 16-17, 87

Texas and Pacific Railway, 63, 75

Texas Highway Department, 87

Texas Historic Cemetery Designation, 155

Texas Observer, 125

Texas State Gazette, 23

Thayer, Ronnie, 144

Thigpen, Drew, 157

Thomas Akers Survey, 36

Thomas, Walter P., 32-33, 179

Thompson, Delia and Harrison, 67

Thorpe, C. T., 97, 166

Thorpe, Dollie Cheney. *See* Cheney, Dollie

Tolliver, Beverly. *See* Sanders, Beverly Tolliver

tornado, xviii, 1, 156-57

Trigg, Gladys. *See* Sanders, Gladys Trigg

Trigg, Inez. *See* Sanders, Inez Trigg

Trigg, Opal. *See* Woods, Opal Trigg

Trinity Cemetery. *See* New Trinity Cemetery

Trinity Chapel Methodist Church and Cemetery, 69

Trinity River, xi, 28-29, 36, 38, 41-42, 44, 60, 75, 78, 86-92, 94, 109, 125, 158-59

Tucker, R. H., 34

TXI (Texas Industries Inc.), 89, 91

Universal Mills, 140, 189

Valley Baptist Church, 66, 110, 113, 119, 142, 145, 157; *xviii, 111, 156*

Veasley, Mr. and Mrs. Will and family, 127
Vienna, Texas, 20
voting, 5, 25, 26, 150

Waggoner, Guy, 171
Walker, Millie and William, 70
Walton, Mr. and Mrs. Pete and family, 127
Walnut Grove School, 70
Warren, Rev. E. E., 113
Washington, James, 144
Watts, Lula V., 127
Weatherd, Mr. and Mrs. Roscoe and family, 127
whiskey-barrel election, 25
White Elephant Saloon, 46
Whitfield, John W., 21
William R. Reeder Survey, 32, 89
Williams, Reece, 113
Williams, Versia L., Elementary School, 73, 129

Wilson, Bit, 114-115
Wilson, Clara Boaz, 29, 168
Wilson, Edward W., 168
Wilson, Ida, 168
Wilson, Isiah, 113
Wilson, Joe, 29, 168
Wilson, Joe F., 168
Wilson, Mr. and Mrs. Lee and family, 127
Windfohr, Robert, 171
Wise, Dennis, 152
Woods, Joe, xiv, 50, 61, 149
Woods, Opal Trigg, xiv, 50, 61, 135-36, 149; 60
Wright, Mr. and Mrs. Clift and family, 127
Wright, Sim, 71

Yams, Aunt Cindy's Candied, 55-56

ABOUT THE AUTHOR

Drew Sanders grew up in the Garden of Eden, where he listened to stories of the early days told by his aunt Doll and grandfather James "Dick Cheney" Sanders. He worked for thirty-eight years for the Fort Worth Sand and Gravel Division of TXI and spent over thirty years researching family history for this book.